William Jessup University
Library
333 Sunset Blvd.
Rocklin, Ca 95765

GETTING ACQUAINTED
WITH THE BIBLE

GETTING ACQUAINTED
WITH THE BIBLE

by

MARTIN HEGLAND, PH.D.

1287

Published by AUGSBURG PUBLISHING HOUSE *Minneapolis*

GETTING ACQUAINTED WITH THE BIBLE

© Augsburg Publishing House, 1936

Sixteenth Printing   October 1959

Manufactured in the United States of America

. . . 5290 . . .

DEDICATED

TO STUDENTS EVERYWHERE WHO
ASPIRE TO FULNESS OF LIFE AND
WHO MAY BE LED TO FIND THE
WAY BY THE REVELATION OF GOD

FOREWORD

AS the title indicates, these study helps are intended to serve as an introduction to the Bible. The plan of the present work, however, differs markedly from most Bible introductions. The usual type presents information *about* the Bible and its various books, that may be read and studied independently of the Bible. These helps aim to lead the student into first-hand contact with the Bible itself. Following the opening chapters, which of necessity deal with facts *about* the Bible, the study suggestions require actual reading and study of the Bible text. The aim is to stimulate through questions and observation notes definitely motivated and intelligent reading to the end that the meanings and messages of the Bible may become luminous and personally helpful to the student. It is hoped that in this way the student may be assisted in obtaining an appreciation of the character of this remarkable Book and in forming a life-long habit of reading and studying its varied contents.

The plan contemplates a course of introductory Bible study that may be completed in a relatively short period of time, and in order to allow as much time as possible for the readings in the Bible the notes of introduction for the several books are cast in brief and outline form. Having pursued this course the student should be ready and eager for more intensive study of the books and themes of the Bible.

It is perhaps unnecessary to say that the author frankly and unequivocally accepts the supernatural character of the Bible and of Christianity. It is assumed throughout that God has at times acted in miraculous ways and through the books of the Bible given revealed truth to men.

No attempt has been made to enter into a consideration of the many questions raised by the Higher Criticism. The scope and purpose of the present study do not allow this. Furthermore, the author holds the position that the view of the Bible held by the best conservative group of Bible students is amply established by competent scholarship.

Taking the Bible as it has come down to us the plan of this study is so to acquaint the student with the Book that he may have a fairly intelligent conception of its structure and contents and some appreciation of its character as the Book of Life.

The author's indebtedness is large. It is impossible to name all the sources of help and suggestion, but to all of them he expresses deep gratitude. Particular appreciation is acknowledged in the case of the following books: Norlie: *The Open Bible,* and *The Outlined Bible;* Sell: *Bible Study by Books;* Torrey: *How to Study the Bible;* Huffman: *A Guide to the Study of the Old and New Testaments;* Brooks: *Summarized Bible;* Macarthur: *Biblical Literature and Its Background;* Keyser: *A System of Christian Evidence;* Wells: *Why We Believe the Bible.*

The execution of the maps is the work of Miss Rachel Lunde.

For helpful criticism and suggestions I make grateful acknowledgement to my wife.

MARTIN HEGLAND.

Northfield, Minnesota, July, 1936.

TABLE OF CONTENTS

CHAPTER I

An Intriguing Prospect

We stand upon the threshold of an enriching experience. We are to undertake an exploration in a profoundly significant field of human interest.

Men of enterprise have repeatedly been willing to risk life and limb in exploration of the frozen regions of the Arctic and of the Antarctic, of the wilds of Africa, and of other remote areas of the earth. By the aid of telescope, microscope, scalpel, and test-tube, scientists have expended untold energy in an effort to uncover the secrets of nature. Archaeologists and historians have been tireless in their search for hidden data of the past. These efforts have all been eminently worth while and productive of valuable knowledge.

In our present enterprise, however, we are undertaking an exploration in fields which in interest and importance for mankind are most basic of all—the fields of religion and morality.

Religion is coextensive with the human race. No people or tribe has anywhere been found that does not possess some form of religion. Dr. Fairbairn says: "Mark!—Man is a religious being. Look to the north and south, the east and west, and what do you see? Religions. Wherever you turn—man; wherever man—religion."

Not only is religion a universal phenomenon, but it constitutes a tremendously powerful factor in human affairs. In the words of Theodore Parker: "The religious sentiment is the strongest and deepest element in human nature." Henry Ward Beecher expressed the same idea: "Religion is but the expression of man's deepest and noblest nature."

There are those who have thought that man will outgrow his religion with increase of knowledge, but, while a man may change his ideas of religion, he cannot get

1

away from religion, because it is a part of his very constitution. As Dr. Love says: "Religion is the one surviving aspect of popular interest in every age. All other questions are issues of the hour. Religion is not custom; it is nature. It will remain a vital question so long as nature and human nature remain unchanged fundamentally." We are reminded of the trenchant words of Sabatier: "Man is incurably religious."

Moral phenomena are also universally met with. Man everywhere has some sense of moral obligation, usually very closely associated with his religious convictions.

In these fields of paramount importance—religion and morality—our present investigation is to be carried on. It is an enterprise that touches every department of our being—that spans the cycles of time and links us with the reaches of eternity.

In our study we shall incidentally touch upon related fields of large human interest. Geographically we shall have to do with lands vitally associated with the career of mankind. In addition to Palestine, our study will bring us into contact with Chaldea, Mesopotamia, Egypt, Arabia, Phoenicia, Babylonia, Persia, Syria, Assyria, Asia Minor, Macedonia, Greece, Rome, and many other lands.

Historically we shall deal with the beginnings of the whole human race; more particularly with the records of a special people, the Israelites, and their contacts with the nations of the world for some two thousand years.

Ethnologically we shall note the origins and distributions of the various races.

Sociologically we shall observe some of the most interesting phenomena ever recorded.

In a legal way we shall mark the foundations upon which civilized law and government have been built.

In a literary way we shall be introduced to matchless classics in history, poetry, prophecy, oratory, drama, and short stories.

All of this and more are in prospect as we set out to get acquainted with that most marvelous of all books, the Bible.

Men of all creeds and shades of opinion have given expression to their admiration for this Book.

In the autumn of 1832 Sir Walter Scott, whose literary fame was world-wide, was lying upon his deathbed at Abbotsford. As a partial relief to his sufferings he requested his son-in-law to read to him.

"What book shall I read?" asked Mr. Lockhart.

"Why do you ask that question?" replied Sir Walter. "There is but one Book; bring me the Bible."

Here are some more evaluations of the Bible by men of note.

Samuel Taylor Coleridge: "For more than a thousand years the Bible, collectively taken, has gone hand in hand with civilization, science, law; in short, with moral and intellectual cultivation; always supporting, and often leading the way. Good and holy men, and the best and wisest of mankind, the kingly spirits of history have borne witness to its influences and have declared it to be beyond compare the most perfect instrument of humanity."

Daniel Webster: "If we abide by the principles taught in the Bible, our country will go on prospering and to prosper; but if we and our posterity neglect its instructions and authority, no man can tell how sudden a catastrophe may overwhelm us and bury all our glory in profound obscurity.

"I have read it through many times; I now make a practice of going through it once a year. It is a book of all others for lawyers as well as divines, and I pity the man who cannot find in it a rich supply of thought and rule for conduct."

Jean Jacques Rousseau: "Peruse the books of philosophers, with all their pomp of diction: how meager, how contemptible are they when compared with the Scriptures! The majesty of the Scriptures strikes me with admiration."

John Quincy Adams: "The first and almost the only book deserving of universal attention is the Bible. I speak as a man of the world to men of the world, and I say to you, 'Search the Scriptures'. The earlier my children begin to read it the more confident will be my hopes that they will prove useful citizens of their country and respectable members of society."

Andrew Jackson: "It is the rock on which our Republic rests."

William McKinley: "The more profoundly we study this wonderful Book, and the more closely we observe its divine precepts, the better citizens we will become and the higher will be our destiny as a Nation."

Theodore Roosevelt: "Almost every man who has by his life-work added to the sum of human achievement of which the race is proud, of which our people are proud, almost every such man has based his life-work largely upon the teachings of the Bible."

Woodrow Wilson: "A man has deprived himself of the best there is in the world who has deprived himself of this [a knowledge of the Bible]. There are a good many problems before the American people today, and before me as President, but I expect to find the solution of those problems just in the proportion that I am faithful in the study of the Word of God. It is very difficult indeed for a man, or for a boy, who knows the Scripture ever to get away from it. It haunts him like an old song. It follows him like the memory of his mother. It forms a part of the warp and woof of his life."

The above statements touch upon the significance of the Bible mainly in its civic and political influence. To the Christian it is of course even more important as a source of spiritual truth leading men into right relations with God and with one another and opening the way to eternal life. From whatever angle we approach the Bible the exploration of its contents offers an intriguing prospect.

CHAPTER II

How the Bible Came to Us

ITS ORIGIN

An abundance of evidence indicates that the various books of the Old Testament were written at different times throughout a period of about a thousand years prior to 400 B. C. In the case of the New Testament the books were written from about 50 A. D. to 100 A. D.

The writers of the books of the Bible were, of course, human beings. But it has always been the historic Christian belief that they wrote under an influence of the Holy Spirit which has been called "Inspiration."

This fact of inspiration makes the Bible qualitatively different from all other books in the world. It is different not merely in degree but in kind. It stands in a class by itself, unique and unparalleled. It is in very truth the Word of God.

HOW THE BOOKS OF THE BIBLE WERE SELECTED

There were many other books in Bible lands than those we find in our present Bible. This was true both in the Old and the New Testament times. How did it come about that just the books that we have were included in the Bible and not others?

The answer in brief is that the selection was made by the spiritual consciousness of godly people. In order to appreciate what this statement means, let us note the activity of the Holy Spirit in the affairs of men. Both Scripture and experience make it abundantly clear that in the lives that are surrendered to God there is definite light and guidance that come from the Holy Spirit. Men become wondrously wise spiritually when they permit Him to instruct them. Jesus spoke of this to His disciples when He assured them of the Spirit's help whenever they came into a difficult situation: "The Holy Spirit shall teach you in that very hour what ye ought to say" (Luke 12:12). And on another occasion He told them that the Holy Spirit "shall guide you into all truth" (John 16:13).

Many of us have been repeatedly amazed at the spirit ual understanding and insight of people who may have had but a meager general education, but who have been in attendance in the school of the Holy Spirit.

This divinely guided consciousness of godly people in Bible times enabled them to judge what was spiritually true and what was false in the books that circulated among them and to detect the evidences of inspiration. There were, to be sure, certain specific standards set up as time went on, such as authorship, time of writing, language used, and the like. But the main fact to bear in mind is that as a result of the operation of the spiritual judgments of godly people there emerged out of the mass of writings certain books which by common agreement were regarded as divinely inspired. These books we call the *Canon* or the *Canonical Books*. "Canon" is a Greek word which means a rule or measuring line. A Canonical book, therefore, is one that conforms to the "Canon," that is, passes the test.

There is much evidence to indicate that the Canon of the Old Testament was fixed by about the year 400 B. C. largely as a result of the work of Ezra and Nehemiah and a council of Jews known as the Great Synagogue, which met after the return from the Babylonian captivity. Long before that time, however, many of the books we now have in the Old Testament had been agreed upon as inspired.

In the case of the New Testament the fixing of the Canon was done mainly at the Council at Carthage in 387 A. D., although the evidence points to the selection of the books as early as about the year 100 A. D.

Certain books known as Apocryphal Books were by some regarded as on a par with the Canonical books, but they were not admitted to the Canon by those who were in the best position to pass on their merits.

How the Books Were Transmitted

There are no original manuscripts of any of the Bible books known to be in existence today. Perhaps God's wisdom is evident in this, for if any of them did exist, some people might be tempted to worship them as idols.

Humanly speaking, the absence of any originals or even of the earliest copies is explainable on the ground of the perishableness of the materials and the Jewish custom not to tolerate any soiled or worn-out copies of their Scriptures. These were either burned or buried.

Since there were no printing presses in Bible times, the various books had to be reproduced by hand. They were written on baked clay tablets, on parchment (sheepskin), on paper made of the papyrus reed, and later on vellum (calfskin). The copying was done with extreme and conscientious care.

"The columns must be of exactly equal length and the words precisely on the line. The letters were carefully counted, and the omission of a single letter from a single word, or even the touching of two letters, would condemn a copy, if it was intended for reading in public worship. And imperfect copies were always destroyed."[1]

In spite of the extreme care exercised in copying the Bible books, minor errors inevitably crept in through the course of the centuries. Hence there arose what are known as *variations* in the manuscripts. A great many of these have been listed, but scholars are of the opinion that not a single variation vitally affects any basic Christian truth.

In order to determine as nearly as possible what the original text was, a vast amount of scholarship has been expended in the study of old manuscripts, early translations, quotations from and references to the Bible in other ancient writings.

---

[1] Wells, *Why We Believe the Bible,* p. 6.

Some very old and valuable manuscripts of the Bible have been found, among them the following:

1) *The Sinaitic manuscript,* discovered in a convent at Mt. Sinai, in 1859, dating from about 330 A. D. It was recently bought from the Russians by the British Museum. It contains all of the New Testament and large portions of the Old.

2) *The Vatican manuscript,* found in Egypt and kept in the Vatican library at Rome. This dates from the middle of the fourth century and contains nearly the entire Bible.

3) *The Alexandrian manuscript* was probably written in Alexandria and belongs to the fifth century. It is preserved in the British Museum.

4) *The Ephraim manuscript* dates also from the fifth century. It was written in Alexandria and derives its name from the fact that some works of the church father Ephraim are written crosswise over it. It is in the National Library in Paris.

5) *The Beza manuscript,* from the fifth century, is named after its discoverer, Theodore Beza, and is in the possession of the library of Cambridge University, England.

6) *The Washington manuscript* is in the Smithsonian Institute. It dates from the fourth or fifth century.

7) *Earlier Fragments.* Recently there have been reported discoveries of small fragments of New Testament manuscripts which seem to date back to near the year 100 A. D.

These early manuscripts are of very large usefulness in helping to determine the original reading of the Bible writings. Other things being equal, the older the manuscript the more nearly it approaches the original.

In addition to the above, thousands of Bible manuscripts have been found, made before the art of printing was introduced by Gutenberg (1438-1450). The first book printed was the Bible.

As a result of able, extensive, and painstaking textual

scholarship it may be confidently affirmed that we possess today the Bible books essentially as they came from the inspired writers.

BIBLE TRANSLATIONS

Most of the books of the Old Testament were written in Hebrew, and most of the New in Greek. In order to make the writings available to people of other languages, translations were made, beginning at an early date and continuing to the present day. A translation of the Old Testament into Greek was made about the year 200 B. C. This is called the *Septuagint* from the circumstance, as tradition has it, that a commission of seventy men was appointed to do the work, *septuaginta* being the Latin word for seventy.

In the Christian era Bible translation got under way very early. Some of the first translations, called versions, are the following:

a) *The Peshitto,* or *Syriac version,* about 150 A. D.
b) *The Itala,* or *Old Latin version,* about 160 A. D.
c) *The Vulgate,* a Latin version by Jerome in the latter part of the fourth century.
d) *The Coptic version* (Old Egyptian) fourth century.
e) *The Ethiopic version,* fourth century.
f) *The Gothic,* fourth century.
g) *The Armenian,* fifth century.

In modern times, the translation by Dr. Martin Luther into German occupies high rank. The New Testament was completed in 1522, and the whole Bible in 1534.

An important early translation into English was that of Tyndale, published in 1525. The first complete English Bible, the work of Coverdale, was published in 1535.

In 1611 was published an English translation of the Bible which is commonly known as the Authorized Version or the King James Version, from the fact that the work was done by a commission appointed by King James I. This version is still in common use and has exercised untold influence upon the diction and style of masters of literature in the English tongue.

A thorough revision of the Authorized Version by English and American scholars was published in 1881, known as the Revised Version. A still more extensive revision by American scholars appeared in 1901. This is known as The American Standard Edition of the Revised Version.

While retaining as much as possible of the beauty of the King James Version, the Revised Version eliminates many archaic expressions, simplifies the language in places, and reproduces more nearly the original. By reason of the fact, too, that the scholars who produced the Revised Version made constant use of some of the oldest known manuscripts, which had not been discovered in the time of King James, they were able to check up on certain variant readings and thus establish more nearly the original text. While many Bible readers prefer the King James Version, the Revised Version is to be recommended, at least for study purposes, because of the facts set forth above.

In recent times several translations by individual scholars have appeared, presenting the Bible in very modern dress. While these versions are often extremely illuminating, they should be used with discrimination because the translations are often very free and sometimes, regrettably, reveal the individual theological bias of the translators. It would appear self evident that a group of able Bible scholars can produce a more correct and satisfactory translation than one done by a single individual.

CHAPTER III

Evidences of the Inspiration of the Bible

Since the question of the character of the Bible is of paramount importance as regards matters of both faith and conduct, and since the supernatural inspiration of the Bible has been vigorously challenged, it is in order for us to give special attention to the problem of the real nature of the Book.

In setting forth what the inspiration of the Bible means we may say that in some instances it includes a supernatural illumination by the Holy Spirit by virtue of which the writers came to know matters that they would not otherwise have known. As, for instance, the predictions of prophecy.

In all instances, whether the contents of their records were received supernaturally or in ordinary ways, inspiration with reference to the Bible means that the writers were supernaturally guided by the Holy Spirit in such ways that the resultant product is in very truth the Word of God.

The actual process of inspiration of the Biblical writings, being supernatural, is, of course, impossible for the human mind fully to understand. Many theories of inspiration have been set forth, which are interesting enough to contemplate. But we need not in this introductory study spend time in more or less fruitless speculations as to the "how" of inspiration.

It is in order, however, to consider some of the reasons why Christians believe that the Bible is inspired.

In dealing with the evidences for the inspiration of the Bible we shall take a broad view of the subject. We shall consider both direct and indirect evidence. For example, we shall admit as relevant to the matter evidences pointing to the accuracy and trustworthiness of the Bible. Now these qualities alone would not necessarily prove inspiration, for a writing may be accurate and reliable without being inspired. On the other hand, a writing could not well be regarded as divinely inspired if it contained essential error, for God is a God of truth. There is, therefore, in the qualities of accuracy and trustworthiness at least presumptive evidence for the inspiration of the Bible.

Again we shall admit as relevant evidence considerations pointing to the truth of Christianity. The Bible is essentially tied up with Christianity. It is in a sense the product of Christianity and at the same time it is the source and norm of the continued life and experiences of Christians. If Christianity, which claims to be a supernatural religion, is true, that fact constitutes tremendously impressive evidence for the truth of the Bible and for its supernatural character.

Without any attempt at differentiation between direct and indirect evidences, we shall proceed to enumerate some of the significant facts which point to the inspiration of the Bible. In the nature of the case, we cannot in this introductory study develop the evidences at any length. We can do little more than list them.

Evidences are usually classified as *Internal* and *External*—that is, evidences to be found within the Bible itself and evidences to be found outside of the Bible. We shall observe this classification; and, believing that in the external evidences we find more readily a common ground of agreement, we shall begin with that division.

I. EXTERNAL EVIDENCES

1. THE CHRISTIAN CHURCH. The church is here, a mighty fact to be reckoned with, an institution numbering some six hundred million members. On the principle of causality the fact of the church requires an adequate explanation. When we consider the humble beginnings of Christianity, its amazingly rapid growth in the face of gigantic obstacles, its survival through centuries of most bitter persecution, its vast missionary expansion through the ages, the preservation of its doctrines and sacramental rites in the midst of conflict, its numbers, vitality, and growth in the present day, we are forced to the conclusion

that it is a more than human institution. And when we find that the development of Christianity stands in a very close relationship to the Bible, we face a most impressive evidence for the divine character of that Book.

2. THE BENEFICENT INFLUENCES OF CHRISTIANITY. Not only has Christianity been a vast factor in the history of the world, but it has, in the main, proved to be a mighty factor for good. With its emphasis on truth, on the value of the individual, and on the law of love, it has been productive of enlightenment, democracy, civil and religious liberty, the abolition of slavery, the welfare of labor, the emancipation of women, opposition to war, the development of the arts and sciences in a thousand ways. In a recent address Dr. Walter A. Judd, of China, said in effect: "One half the world is illiterate. It is that half that does not know Christ. Is that an accident? One half the world holds a base view of women. It is that half that does not know Christ. Is that an accident? One half of the world has no doctors. It is that half that does not know Christ. Is that an accident? More than all else the world needs Christ."

A religion and a Book that have greatly blessed mankind give evidence of divinity.

3. ARCHAEOLOGY. Vast researches in Bible lands have brought to light materials that have verified the Bible account at a multitude of points where its accuracy had previously been challenged, and at no point have authenticated archaeological finds proved the Bible to be in error. Let a single instance of archaeological verification suffice. In the book of Exodus we are told that the Egyptians compelled the Israelites to work as slaves in construction work, part of which was the erection of storehouses in the city of Pithom. To begin with they were provided with straw as binding material in making bricks; as oppression grew, the Israelites were compelled to go out into the fields and gather their own straw; finally they were compelled to make bricks without straw. In 1883 the ruins of Pithom were excavated; and in 1908, the

noted archaeologist, Professor Kyle, wrote about the ruins:

"The bricks are laid in mortar contrary to the usual Egyptian custom and contrary to the observation of explorers in Egypt previous to the time of Naville's discovery at Pithom. The lower courses in at least some of the store-chamber work are laid with brick filled with good chopped straw; the upper courses made of brick having in them no binding material whatever, and the middle courses are made of brick filled with stubble pulled up by the roots. The impress of the roots is as plainly marked in the brick as though cut by an engraver's tools."[1]

4. ANCIENT WRITINGS OUTSIDE OF THE BIBLE. Facts of the Bible and early Christianity are mentioned in many non-Biblical writings even within the first and second centuries of the Christian era. Some of these writers and writings are as follows: The Syrian Epistle of Mora; The Jewish historian Josephus; the Romans: Tacitus, Pliny, Hadrian, Marcus Aurelius, and Celsus; the Greek Lucian; the Christians: Clement of Rome, Ignatius of Antioch, The Teachings of the Twelve Apostles, Polycarp, Barnabas of Alexandria, Shephard of Hermas, Papias, Epistle of Mathetes, Justin Martyr, Marcion, and Irenaeus.

5. THE FULFILLMENT OF PROPHECY. The Bible contains great numbers of predictions of future events, many of which were fulfilled to the last detail hundreds of years afterwards. Practically every phase of the life of Christ was prophesied in the Old Testament. Prophecies have been fulfilled in the case of Palestine, Egypt, Babylonia, Tyre, Sidon, Edom, Philistia, and many other lands. The conditions existing today in these countries are in many respects in striking agreement with the prophetic utterances in the Bible. Perhaps the most amazing instance is the present state of the Jewish people, scattered over the face of the earth, possessing no national home and yet

[1] Kyle, *Moses and the Monuments*, p. 156.

preserving their racial and religious identity, all in perfect accord with prophecy. By no possible stretch of the imagination can it be assumed that the many fulfilled prophecies are the result of guess work. They bear unmistakable evidence of divine inspiration.

6. COMPARISON WITH THE SACRED BOOKS OF OTHER RELIGIONS. Many of the other religions of the world have their sacred books containing systems of theology and ethics. In these writings are found many wise sayings and beautiful ideas, often mingled, however, with grotesque and offensive features. Compared with these other sacred books the Bible is unique in its central character, Christ, in its system of redemption, and in the purity of its ethics —facts that point definitely to a divine origin.

7. BIBLE TRANSLATIONS AND SALES. In the midst of a multitude of new books pouring from the printing presses of the world the Bible continues to be by far the best seller. Into about a thousand languages and dialects the Bible has been translated, a record far surpassing that of any other book. The demand for the Bible is so great that in some instances printing presses are running night and day to meet the requirements. And this after the enemies of the Bible have done everything in their power to discredit it and to prevent its circulation. There must be something more than human about such a book.

8. CHRISTIAN EXPERIENCE. Speaking of the teachings which He brought from His Father, Jesus said: "If any man willeth to do his will, he shall know of the teaching, whether it is of God, or whether I speak from myself" (John 7:17). Millions of people have tried this test and have found that Christ's teachings, when followed, do produce a result in Christian experience. The effects which the Bible claims to produce have been experienced over and over again through the Christian centuries. Human wrecks have been lifted out of the gutter and restored to upright manhood and womanhood; agnostics and atheists who have permitted the words of the Bible to work upon their minds and hearts have come through to

a triumphant Christian faith; weak men and women have by the use of the Book been sustained in the face of soul-testing temptations; earnest Christian souls have grown mightily in grace and holiness by feeding upon the words of the Book. And the miracles of changed and transformed lives continue today. Christian experiences throughout the world, wherever the Bible touches human lives, constitute a clinching proof of its divine character.

CHAPTER IV

Internal Evidences of the Inspiration of the Bible

Having examined briefly some of the evidences outside of the Bible which point to its divine inspiration, let us now look into the Bible itself to see whether or not we find there any marks of a divine character. Here, too, we can do little more than list the items we find.

1. THE BIBLE'S OWN CLAIMS. Repeatedly throughout the Bible there is recorded the fact that God made facts known to His people. Some of the expressions frequently met with are as follows: "God called unto him and said," "The Lord saith," "The Lord spoke," "The word of God came." It has been computed that these and similar expressions occur about two thousand times in the Bible. Here is a sample instance: "These are the words of the covenant which Jehovah commanded Moses to make with the children of Israel in the land of Moab, besides the covenant which he made with them in Horeb" (Deut. 29:1).

The fact of divine inspiration is definitely taught in the following passage by Paul: "All scripture is given by inspiration of God and is profitable for doctrine, for reproof, for correction, for instruction in righteousness" (2 Tim. 3:16).

Another equally specific passage is from Peter's Second Epistle: "And we have the word of prophecy made more sure; whereunto ye do well that ye take heed, as unto a lamp shining in a dark place, until the day dawn, and the day-star arise in your hearts: knowing this first, that no prophecy of scripture is of private interpretation. For no prophecy ever came by the will of man: but men spake from God, being moved by the Holy Spirit" (II Peter 1:19-21).

2. THE UNITY AND CONSISTENCY OF THE BIBLE. In spite of the fact that the Bible consists of 66 separate books, written over a period of some 1500 years, by about 40 different authors of widely different training and geographical distribution, the Bible constitutes an amazing unity from beginning to end, centering about the exalted theme: *Redemption through Christ.* In the Old Testament we meet it in types and prophecies; in the New, in fulfillment.

Someone has said: "Cut the Bible at any point, and it will bleed." It is a unified living organism with life-blood running through its every part.

Every part of the Bible, when rightly understood, is in agreement with every other part both in doctrine and ethics. This remarkable unity and consistency of the Bible point unmistakably to a single source, God Himself.

3. THE HISTORICAL CHARACTER OF THE BIBLE. Throughout many of its books the Bible presumes to record historical data. It gives the distinct impression that it is not dealing with myths or legends but with historical facts. It records with utmost preciseness geographical locations, names of countries and rulers, and the details of events.

Note the careful approach of Luke to the writing of his Gospel: "Forasmuch as many have taken in hand to draw up a narrative concerning those matters which have been fulfilled among us, even as they delivered them unto us, who from the beginning were eyewitnesses and ministers of the word, it seemed good to me also, having traced the course of all things accurately from the first, to write unto thee in order, most excellent Theophilus; that thou mightest know the certainty concerning the things wherein thou wast instructed" (Luke 1:1-4).

Note also the care with which he fixes the time and place of the beginning of John's ministry: "Now in the fifteenth year of the reign of Tiberius Caesar, Pontius Pilate being governor of Judaea, and Herod being tetrarch of Galilee, and his brother Philip tetrarch of the region of Ituraea and Trachonitis, and Lysanias tetrarch of

Abilene, in the high-priesthood of Annas and Caiaphas, the word of God came unto John the son of Zacharias in the wilderness. And he came into all the region round about the Jordan, preaching the baptism of repentance unto remission of sins" (Luke 3:1-3).

Does this read like a record of myths?

The above are but samples of a host of passages that might be cited to show the conscientiousness of the careful historian.

4. THE FRANKNESS AND REALISM OF THE BIBLE. With no attempt to gloss over unpleasant things, the Bible pictures facts just as they are. Sin and righteousness alike are presented with the utmost realism. In fact, the Bible has been accused of immorality because of the unvarnished accounts of sin and ungodliness which it at times presents. But it tells the truth. If the accounts were fictitious, they would not have included the ugly chapters in the lives of heroes as for instance in the case of Abraham, Jacob, Moses, and David. Its very frankness is an evidence of the veracity of the Bible.

5. THE BIBLE FITS HUMAN NEEDS. Dr. Leander S. Keyser, in his *System of Christian Evidences,* says of this characteristic of the Bible:

a) "It satisfies man's natural longing for God.

b) "It complements the conscious weakness of human nature by its doctrine of regeneration.

c) "The desire for positive assurance of truth is met in the teaching of the Bible.

d) "The Bible affords comfort in every kind of trial.

e) "It gives promise of the solution, either in time or in eternity, of all human problems.

f) "The universal desire to be right with God, without violation of the law of justice, is satisfied through the mediation of Christ.

g) "Christianity meets the desire of the soul for inner purity.

h) "Christianity cancels the fear of death and satisfies the hope and the desire for immortality."

19

6. THE UP-TO-DATENESS OF THE BIBLE. Though its last books were written about eighteen centuries ago, the Bible impresses one as being a contemporary book. Many books are out-of-date almost before they are printed. The Bible holds its place through the centuries. This can only be accounted for on the ground that the Bible deals with truths that are permanent and absolute and do not change with the passing of time.

7. THE CHARACTER OF THE APOSTLES. Much of the New Testament was written by the Apostles of Jesus as eye-witnesses of the events they record. All the evidence indicates that these men were sober, truthful, practical, competent, and responsible individuals, such as would make good witnesses in any court room. Some critics have charged them with being credulous, ready to believe anything; but the record indicates quite the contrary. They were in fact slow to believe and had to have conclusive evidence to be convinced of the truth of any matter. Witness, for instance, the attitude and demand of Thomas in regard to the resurrection of Christ: "Except I shall see in his hands the print of the nails, and put my finger into the print of the nails, and put my hand into his side, I will not believe" (John 20:25).

8. THE CONVERSION AND CAREER OF THE APOSTLE PAUL. The conversion of Paul was an event most unlikely to occur. He was a distinctly intellectual type, highly educated. He honestly believed that Christianity was false and that he was doing God a well-pleasing service in persecuting the Christians. Something extraordinary must have happened to change the whole outlook and career of such a strong character. He himself attributes the change to a vision of Christ. Paul was so intellectually keen that when he saw Christ alive, he realized instantly that Christianity was true and that he himself had been on the wrong track. There is no possible way of explaining the conversion of Paul except by this conviction; and the record shows that the conviction was produced by supernatural means.

Also, the career of Paul is a powerful evidence of the

truth of Christianity and the Bible. His indefatigable missionary labors, his willingness to endure all manner of hardships, suffering, and persecution for Christ's sake, his clear-cut evangelical preaching, his illuminating epistles, and his masterly exposition of Christian doctrine are inexplicable on any other premise than that Christianity is true.

9. THE CHARACTER AND WORDS OF JESUS. We have reserved for last treatment this item, for it constitutes the crucial and paramount evidence of the supernatural character of the Bible.

There is practically universal agreement among all students of the life of Jesus that His character is the most superlatively excellent met with in all history. In moral purity, in loving kindness, in spiritual insight, in poised dignity, in fearless courage, in unruffled calmness, in tireless patience He stands unique and unparalleled. Here are some estimates of Jesus by men of renown:

David Frederich Strauss, German rationalistic theologian: "Christ stands alone, and unapproached in the world's history. He remains the highest model of religion within the reach of our thought. No perfect piety is possible without His presence in the heart."

Charles H. Spurgeon, English clergyman: "Christ is the great central fact in the world's history. To Him everything looks forward or backward. All the lines of history converge upon Him. All the great purposes of God culminate in Him. The greatest and most momentous fact which the history of the world records is the fact of His birth."

Granted the uniquely superlative character of Jesus, special importance attaches to His words in several respects.

What did Jesus think about the Old Testament, the Bible of His day?

Certainly that question should be of large interest. In point of time He was about nineteen hundred years nearer to it than we are. And if He was God, as He claimed to be, He certainly would know whether or not it was reliable and true. If He had known it to be untrustworthy or fraudulent, it would have been His plain duty to say so. If the people of His time were deluded as to their Scriptures, nothing could have excused Jesus for leaving them in their delusion. He came to proclaim the Truth. Jesus' attitude towards the Old Testament is therefore of profound concern in the determining of our attitude.

Now, what was His attitude? We are not left in doubt on this point, for the Gospel records are full of Jesus' references to contents of the Old Testament books. Let us look at some of them.

1) In a preliminary way we may note that not in a single instance did Jesus suggest a shadow of suspicion that the Old Testament was not a true record. Not once did the expression of a doubt pass His lips.

2) At least 55 times, as recorded in the Gospels, not counting duplications, Jesus made definite reference to matters contained in the Old Testament books in such a way as to give the definite impression that He regarded those records as authentic.

3) He referred by name to the following persons: Abel, Noah, Abraham, Lot, Isaac, Jacob, Moses, David, Solomon, Elijah, Elisha, Naaman, Isaiah, Jonah, Zachariah, Daniel.

4) He mentioned the following events or facts: The Flood, destruction of Sodom and Gomorrah, the burning bush, manna in the wilderness, the giving of the Law, the brazen serpent, David's eating of show-bread, arrayal of Solomon, visit of the queen of Sheba, drought in the days of Elijah, cleansing of the leper Naaman, repentance of the inhabitants of Nineveh, death of Zachariah.

5) He affirmed the fulfillment of prophecies in at least twenty instances.

6) At least fifteen times He appealed to passages in the Old Testament in defense of statements or practices.

7) Three times, at least, He affirmed the absolute finality of "Scripture." In the "Sermon on the Mount" He said: "Think not that I am come to destroy the law, or the prophets. I am not come to destroy, but to fulfill. For

verily I say unto you, Till heaven and earth pass, one jot or one tittle shall in no wise pass from the law, till all be fulfilled" (Matt. 5:17-18).

On another occasion He said: "Scripture cannot be broken" (John 10:35). And again: "It is easier for heaven and earth to pass away, than for one tittle of the law to fall" (Luke 16:17).

8) As an illustration of how Jesus regarded the Old Testament let us note two passages recorded by Luke. It was in the evening of resurrection day. Jesus drew near to two men walking to Emmaus. He entered into conversation with them, and discovering that they were greatly perplexed about the things that had lately transpired in Jerusalem, He said: "O fools, and slow of heart to believe all that the prophets have spoken: Ought not Christ to have suffered these things, and to enter into his glory? And beginning at Moses and the prophets, he expounded unto them in all the scriptures the things concerning himself" (Luke 24:25-27).

Later the same day, appearing among the Disciples in the upper room, He said to them: "These are the words which I spake unto you, while I was yet with you, that all things must be fulfilled, which were written in the law of Moses, and in the prophets, and in the psalms, concerning me. Then opened he their understanding, that they might understand the scriptures. And said unto them, Thus it is written, and thus it behoved Christ to suffer, and to rise from the dead the third day: and that repentance and remission of sins should be preached in his name among all nations, beginning at Jerusalem. And ye are witnesses of these things" (Luke 24:44-48).

Could anything be more definite than this statement? Jesus here affirms without qualification that throughout the law of Moses, the prophets, and the psalms—in other words, throughout the whole of the Old Testament Scriptures—there were prophecies concerning Himself that had been fulfilled. Nothing could more clearly express Jesus' view of the Scriptures of His day.

Summing it all up, what does the evidence point to?

It can lead to no other conclusion than this, that Jesus unquestionably regarded the Old Testament Scriptures as true, historical, authentic, and authoritative.

And what does that mean for us? It should settle the question for us. We make no mistake when we take our stand with Jesus in His attitude that the Old Testament writings are altogether true. And if they are true, they must be inspired, for they contain many things which could not be known or written by human beings except through the illumination and guidance of the Holy Spirit.

But what about the New Testament? That was not yet written in Jesus' time. Did Jesus say anything that may serve as support for the inspiration of the New Testament writings?

We find a very positive answer to this question in Jesus' words about the illumination and guidance which He promised should come from the activity of the Holy Spirit.

1) In times of persecution and trials the Spirit would give believers definite instruction as to what to say: "And when they bring you before the synagogues, and the rulers, and the authorities, be not anxious how or what ye shall answer, or what ye shall say: for the Holy Spirit shall teach you in that very hour what ye ought to say" (Luke 12:11-12).

2) Guidance into truth and the stimulation of memory were to be results of the Spirit's work: "And I will pray the Father, and he shall give you another Comforter, that he may be with you for ever, even the Spirit of truth: whom the world cannot receive; for it beholdeth him not, neither knoweth him: ye know him; for he abideth with you, and shall be in you" (John 14:16-17). "But the Comforter, even the Holy Spirit, whom the Father will send in my name, he shall teach you all things, and bring to your remembrance all that I said unto you" (John 14:26).

3) And in a most remarkable passage the continued functioning of the Holy Spirit in the life of the Apostles and of the church is set forth: "I have yet many things to say unto you, but ye cannot bear them now. Howbeit

when he, the Spirit of truth is come, he shall guide you into all the truth: for he shall not speak from himself; but what things soever he shall hear, these shall he speak: and he shall declare unto you the things that are to come" (John 16:12-13).

We may certainly conclude then that, when the authors of New Testament writings engaged in so supremely important a work as to set down a written record of the life of Christ and the history of the early church, and to instruct individuals and congregations in vital matters of faith and works, they had the full benefit of that supernatural spiritual help which Jesus had promised them in connection with the gift of the Holy Spirit.

Let this be borne in mind, too, that the Holy Spirit is true God, one of the three persons of the Trinity, and as such His words spoken through the instrumentality of attuned and obedient personalities are just as authoritative as are the words of Jesus Himself. It is quite the fashion in certain circles to belittle the words of the Apostles in comparison with the words of Jesus. Not so when the Holy Spirit was ever present to teach them what to say and write, as Jesus definitely foretold.

The answer to our inquiry is clear. In Jesus' promises regarding the Holy Spirit's activity we have definite support for the supernatural inspiration of New Testament writings.

CHAPTER V

The Bible and Science

Some people are greatly disturbed by difficulties encountered in Bible study. Such difficulties should not surprise us. They are in the main due to the partial character of our knowledge and insight. We believe the Bible to be the revelation of God to men, and we should rather expect that it is not easy for finite minds to grasp the thoughts of the Infinite.

Furthermore, the fact that we cannot solve a certain problem arising in Bible study does not mean that scholars of larger knowledge cannot solve it, now or in the future.

Frequently the assertion is made that there is a conflict between science and the Bible. Is this so?

At the risk of being misunderstood, we answer this question by saying: Yes, there is a conflict between science and the Bible. We may go further and say that it would be surprising if there were no conflict.

Are not these strange statements? What do they mean? Let us see.

We Christians believe that God has spoken to the world through two books: the book of His work, which is nature, and the book of His Word, which is the Bible. Consequently, we believe that both of these books are true and that they are in the most beautiful harmony.

But the trouble with us human beings is that our knowledge and understanding of these books is partial and incomplete. Certainly many of our ideas in the two realms are in perfect harmony, but to assert that there is no conflict between our scientific ideas and Bible ideas is equivalent to asserting that all of our ideas in the two realms are altogether and ultimately true.

This assumption, that all the ideas we possess are altogether and ultimately true, it is impossible to maintain. Certainly in the study of nature past history demonstrates that over and over again many scientific explanations have been changed to include new knowledge. Even many ideas that were held to be final by practically universal consent have been discarded as inadequate. Is it reasonable then to assume that all scientific ideas held today are altogether and ultimately true? First-rate scientists themselves are the last people to make such claims. In fact, many scientists contend that we cannot be sure that any of our present scientific ideas are altogether true. Leading scientists, therefore, hesitate to speak of the "assured results" or the "proved theories" of science as confidently as they once did. Instead they warn against dogmatism in science.

Does this mean that science is to be discredited? By no means. Science makes large use of the hypothesis, which may be defined as "A tentative theory or supposition provisionally adopted to explain certain facts, and to guide in the investigation of others."

If the hypothesis is useful in the above respects, it is a valuable hypothesis and serves to stimulate scientific progress even if it should ultimately prove to be a wrong idea or only partially true. In fact, we may say that scientists are not so much concerned with the ultimate truth of the hypothesis itself as with its serviceableness as a tool in scientific investigations. Many hypothesis have proved immensely stimulating in advancing scientific research and in increasing scientific knowledge even though they have ultimately been discarded in the light of fuller knowledge.

Scientists should therefore not be held up to scorn because they have for a time held to a hypothesis which they later have found necessary to abandon or modify. In the meantime they may have made large progress. The new hypothesis usually represents an advance over the old.

The mischief is, of course, that many second rate scientists speak of certain hypotheses and theories as if they were ultimately and eternally established as true and as if there could not possibly be any doubt in regard to them any more. Such scientists are real trouble makers, and not least for science itself.

So far in our discussion attention has been directed to the incompleteness of knowledge and the consequent tentative character of many hypotheses in the field of science. How is it with our knowledge of the Bible? Are we sure that all the ideas which we today say the Bible teaches are altogether true? Here, too, history should make us cautious. There was a time when it was held that the Bible teaches that the earth is flat, and anyone who believed or taught otherwise was branded as a heretic.

Does this mean that we cannot be sure and definite about our Christian faith? By no means. In his explanation of the Catechism, Pontoppidan makes a wondrously wise statement that is pertinent in this connection. He says, in free translation: "In all the matters necessary to know for salvation the Bible is clear enough for him who rightly uses it, whether he be a layman or a scholar." The great Bible truths such as those about God, creation, sin, redemption through Christ, grace, and our eternal destiny, we may hold to with abounding confidence as being the clear revelations of God, transcending the limitations of the human mind in its feeble search for truth. But in regard to some of the non-essential questions in dispute, duly recognizing the fact that "now we see through a glass darkly" and that we "know in part," it is becoming of us to speak guardedly. Christians have nothing to lose, but much to gain by such an attitude of modesty. The most profound Bible scholars have been the most ready to admit their limitations in the field of Bible knowledge.

Now then, let us get back to our original question about the conflict between science and the Bible.

We may ask: On account of our admittedly partial knowledge and limited insight, both in regard to nature and the Bible, is it at all surprising if there is conflict between our present ideas in these two realms?

If some of our present ideas are erroneous—an assumption which is altogether reasonable, as we have seen—there is bound to be conflict. To insist that there should be complete harmony, would be to require all our present ideas in both spheres to be altogether true and correct. Such a requirement it is impossible to meet when we take into account the often fumbling efforts of our darkened understanding in its search for truth. Why not recognize as a fact what is a fact, namely that our present knowledge and insight are partial, and possibly erroneous, in some cases?

Why then be so greatly concerned about harmonizing our present partial, and perhaps faulty, ideas of nature and the Bible? If we do the job after a fashion, today, we shall have to do it over again tomorrow, when new elements are introduced into the equation.

What attitude, then, shall we take to this whole question?

Let scientists proceed on their way, learning everything they possibly can from the book of nature. Let them gather data, analyze and compare facts, advance hypotheses, and proceed to verification and generalization, all in the spirit of those great noblemen of science whose attitude is well expressed by one who said, "I bow before the mystery concealed in a bit of living protoplasm." Let the church bestow its sincere blessings upon the true scientists who launch out upon an unbiased search for truth. None are more hostile to error or more eager for the light than they. History shows that science provides correctives for its own errors.

Let us rest assured that no harm can possibly come to God's other Book, the Bible, from real truth discovered in the book of nature. When a scientific hypothesis is advanced, however, that contradicts the Bible, as at present understood, Christians have not only the right but also the obligation to insist that such hypotheses shall not be paraded as fact so long as there are grave differences of opinion among scientists themselves as to the truth of the hypothesis. Vast harm to the faith of young people has often been done by presenting as scientific finalities hypotheses that later have been abandoned. The way in which certain phases of the evolutionary hypothesis have been handled is an illustration in point.

If a certain hypothesis that seems to contradict the Bible is finally found to be unquestionably true, the conflict may possibly be removed, as has happened in the past, by a readjustment of current ideas about what the Bible teaches. At any rate, in the mind of God we know there is perfect harmony.

In the meantime let scientific investigators be wary of what they claim for their hypotheses.

Let students of the Bible, too, proceed to learn everything they possibly can from and about that Book. With prayer for the guidance of the Holy Spirit, without which the revelations of God are incapable of understanding, let Bible students make use of every instrumentality for discovering its true meanings, such as language study, archaeology, history, both sacred and secular, exegesis, and correct principles of interpretation. The more perfectly we know the Bible, the more beautifully and harmoniously God's great thoughts stand revealed.

Summing it all up, we may put it this way: The reason we have difficulties is not that we know so much, but that we know so little. Let us be eager, therefore, for more light from whatever source it may come. And let us take assurance from this consideration that while we may not here be able to put together completely the great puzzle picture of the universe, we shall some day, in God's own time, see all things clearly and in the most beautiful harmony, when we shall see Him "face to face."

CHAPTER VI
Methods of Bible Study

Various ways of reading and studying the Bible have been tried, each of which possesses certain advantages. Some of the methods are the following:

I. READING THE BIBLE THROUGH FROM GENESIS TO REVELATION. This gives an idea of the Bible as a whole in its organic unity and serves as a corrective against onesidedness and lack of balance which might develop through reading only favorite passages.

II. CHAPTER SUMMARY METHOD. This plan involves the analysis and summary of each chapter of the books of the Bible in terms of some such headings as the following:

1. Contents
2. Characters
3. Conclusion
4. Key Word
5. Strong Verses
6. Striking Facts.

The *Summarized Bible* by Keith L. Brooks is a good illustration of this type of Bible study.

III. TOPICAL STUDY. Searching the Bible to discover what it has to say on a certain subject or series of subjects is exceedingly profitable. As an aid in this study the student should use a Bible Concordance or Topical Text-book.

IV. BIOGRAPHICAL STUDY. The Bible may be studied for the light it throws upon the lives of the men and women it portrays. In this plan it is interesting not only to note the biographical facts but also to analyze the character of the person under consideration, giving attention to elements of strength or weakness, difficulties faced, successes attained, and the lessons that may be learned.

V. STUDY FOR PRACTICAL USE. In the important work of soul winning it is essential to know the Bible in such a way as to be able to use its truths effectively with individuals. This involves discovering, selecting, and memorizing key passages of strategic value.

VI. STUDY OF INDIVIDUAL BOOKS. Since the Bible is in reality a collection of books it is self-evident that the study of each book as a unit constitutes a natural and significant method of approach. Book studies may be carried on in a variety of ways. One may gather information about a book in the Bible from treatises by Bible scholars. But one may also go directly to the Book and make a cursory or intensive study of its contents at first hand. In such a plan attention may be given to the authorship, time and circumstances of the writing, general contents, divisions, teachings, and practical lessons to be learned and applied.

VII. THE METHOD OF THE PRESENT STUDY. The Bible study helps outlined in this book involve elements of several of the plans outlined above. Following brief notes on the Bible as a whole and on the Old Testament the method followed is mainly that of studying book by book with such historical and other notes as may be necessary to an understanding of the materials dealt with. The more extensive studies outlined involve reading large portions of the books and making notations in accordance with the study suggestions offered. These study helps have grown out of several years of class-room experience, and it has been found that the best results are obtained if the students keep notebooks in which they enter answers to questions asked under the head of "Study Suggestions."

The plan requires considerable time. If such length of time is not available, briefer methods can, of course, be used. Under the head of "Additional Study Suggestions" alternative or supplementary methods are briefly indicated.

Every study period should be begun with prayer for the illumination and guidance of the Holy Spirit, for a mind open to receive truth, for a conscience sensitive to the messages of the Word, and for a will ready to do the Lord's bidding.

The Bible student will be greatly aided in his work by the use of a good Bible Dictionary and Concordance.

CHAPTER VII

The Bible As a Whole

Having surveyed the general introductory material in the foregoing chapters we proceed now to a consideration of specific facts about the Bible and its structure.

NAME.—The name Bible is derived from the Greek word *biblos,* meaning *book.*

DIVISIONS.—The Bible has two main divisions: the *Old Testament* of 39 books and the *New Testament* of 27 books, making 66 books in all. (As an aid to the memory note this relationship: $3 \times 9 = 27$.)

WRITERS.—The total number of writers is about 40, and they represent a wide range of rank and occupations: kings, priests, prophets, poets, apostles, shepherds, farmers, fishermen, and many others.

THEME.—The theme of the Bible is *Salvation through Christ.* This exalted theme runs through the Bible from beginning to end and constitutes a bond uniting its various parts into a harmonious whole.

CONTENTS.—While presented in greatly varied forms the Bible is essentially the record of God's dealings with men and His revelation to them of His plan for their redemption through Christ and of His will for their living together as His children.

As an aid to getting a whole view of the Bible think of it in terms of the following outline:

THE BIBLE

Theme: Salvation through Christ			
Old Testament	Gospels	Acts and Epistles	Revelation
Preparation of Salvation	Realization of Salvation	Application of Salvation	Culmination of Salvation

33

CHAPTER VIII

The Old Testament

WRITERS.—About 30.

PERIOD OF TIME COVERED.—From the beginning to about 400 B. C.

THEME.—The preparation of salvation through Christ.

GENERAL CONTENTS.—Sketches from the history of humanity up to the time of Abraham, and episodes in the history of Israel from that time on until after the return of the Jews from the exile in Babylon, or until about 400 B. C. In addition the Old Testament contains a wealth of spiritual riches in the form of law, poetry, and prophecy. The idea of the coming Messiah is developed throughout. It begins in a dim way in Genesis, grows more clear as time goes on, until in the prophets it is visioned forth in definite form.

THE BOOKS AND THEIR GROUPINGS.—The books of the Old Testament may be grouped as follows:

A. Historical—17 books.

    1. Genesis   ⎤
    2. Exodus   ⎥ The Pentateuch,
    3. Leviticus   ⎬ meaning
    4. Numbers   ⎥ five books
    5. Deuteronomy ⎦
    6. Joshua
    7. Judges
    8. Ruth
    9. I Samuel
    10. II Samuel
    11. I Kings
    12. II Kings
    13. I Chronicles
    14. II Chronicles
    15. Ezra
    16. Nehemiah
    17. Esther

34

B. Poetical—5 books.

1. Job
2. Psalms
3. Proverbs
4. Ecclesiastes
5. Song of Solomon

C. Prophetical—17 books.

1. Isaiah
2. Jeremiah
3. Lamentations — Major—5 Books
4. Ezekiel
5. Daniel
6. Hosea
7. Joel
8. Amos
9. Obadiah
10. Jonah
11. Micah — Minor—12 Books
12. Nahum
13. Habakkuk
14. Zephaniah
15. Haggai
16. Zechariah
17. Malachi

BIBLE CHRONOLOGY

The method of reckoning time in ancient history is not clearly known, nor was it uniform in different countries. There is, therefore, considerable divergence of opinion among scholars as to exact dates. The Bible chronology that gained most general acceptance was that worked out by Archbishop Ussher in 1659. As a result of archaeological research and further study, however, competent scholars have come to hold grave doubts as to the correctness of Ussher's dates at many points.

In this study we shall not greatly concern ourselves with the problems of chronology. In some instances when dates are given, remarks are offered as to various views held by different chronologists. As research continues a larger measure of agreement will no doubt be reached.

We shall not concern ourselves with any specific dates before the time of Abraham.

CHAPTER IX

Genesis: A Book of Beginnings

NAME.—The name *Genesis* literally means *beginning* or *birth*. It is therefore a suitable title for the first book in the Bible which tells of the creation of the universe and of many other beginnings.

AUTHOR.—The book of Genesis and the other four books of the Pentateuch have by tradition been ascribed to Moses as author. The Mosaic authorship has been frequently and sharply challenged, but a wealth of scholarly opinion holds to the idea that Moses was the author of all these books with the exception of certain very minor portions which were apparently added by a later writer.

PERIOD OF TIME COVERED.—From the Creation of the world to the death of Joseph.

NUMBER OF CHAPTERS.—50.

CONTENTS.—Beginning with the account of Creation Genesis records various episodes in the early history of humanity in general. With the calling of Abraham it takes up the special phase of sacred history that centers around the chosen people, Israel, and carries the account through the period of the Patriarchs.

OUTLINE OF GENESIS

General Contents:				Some Early History	
Episodes from Primeval History				Episodes from Patriarchal History	
Creation c. 1-2	Fall c. 3-4	Deluge c. 5-9	List of Nations c. 10-11	Abraham —Isaac c. 12-27	Jacob— Joseph c. 28-50

STUDY SUGGESTIONS

With the above facts in mind let us proceed to a brief study of Genesis. It is a good plan in Bible study to read through a book first for a general impression. If the book is too long for such reading within the time available, a certain section should be read as a unit. After such first reading the student should go back and note certain significant passages more particularly. The study suggestions below are grouped in divisions in harmony with the outline of Genesis and are intended as aids to thoughtful reading.

A. EPISODES FROM PRIMEVAL HISTORY. Chapter 1-11.

I. CREATION—Chapters 1-2

1. "In the beginning God"—Let us pause here for a moment. Here we find an answer to some of the problems that philosophers have speculated about through all the ages. As the first clear note of the overture to a great symphony we meet here in this brief and exalted declaration a statement not only of the existence of God but also of His existence before the beginning of time. A necessary logical inference is that God is self-existent, uncaused, eternal, and infinite.

2. Read again v. 1. Note the plain statement assigning the existence of the heavens and the earth to the creative act of God. Clearly, matter is not eternal, but created in time.

3. Note the cosmic sweep of the description in v. 2.

4. List the order of events in the creation account.

5. What is distinctive in the account of the creation of man? See 1:27.

6. Note that Chapter 1 contains an account of creation in general, whereas Chapter 2 tells of the creation of man in greater fullness.

7. Of how many things is the "beginning" recorded in these two chapters?

NOTE ON EVOLUTION.—The term *evolution* is used in many different senses, some absolutely contradictory to the creation account in Genesis and some that perhaps can be harmonized with it. As pointed out in a previous chapter, it is not particularly profitable to try to harmonize in detail the Bible and science because of the admittedly incomplete character of our present knowledge. What we as believers in the Bible insist upon, however, is the conviction that God is the Author of creation, not only in the beginning but all along the line.

37

Among the many illuminating books on evolution written from a Christian point of view may be mentioned the following:

Bettex: *Science and Christianity.*
Fairhurst: *Organic Evolution Considered.*
Graebner: *Creation ex Nihilo.*
Keyser: *The Problem of Origins.*
Mauro: *Evolution at the Bar.*
Nelson: *After Its Kind.*
O'Toole: *The Case Against Evolution.*
Patterson: *The Other Side of Evolution.*
Price: *Q. E. D. New Light on the Doctrine of Creation.*

II. THE FALL INTO SIN—Chapters 3-4

1. In what did Eve's sin chiefly consist?

2. What was the basic cause of the fear referred to in 3:8 and 3:10?

3. What common human trait is revealed in 3:12 and 3:13?

4. What were the consequences of the fall into sin?

5. Gen. 3:15 contains the first prophecy recorded in the Bible of the coming of Jesus Christ as the Savior of the world. The "seed" of the woman indicates the human phase of His origin; "thou shalt bruise his heel" suggests His suffering; while "it shall bruise thy head" predicts His complete victory over Satan. This verse marks the beginning of God's revelation of His plan of Redemption.

6. Note in 3:21 that God made clothing of skins for Adam and Eve. This covering of their nakedness required the death of animals and may be taken as a type of the salvation through Christ which required His death and which covers our sinfulness.

7. Why was not Cain's offering acceptable to the Lord?

8. Note how sin is already taking its toll in the murder of Abel.

9. What are some modern illustrations of the spirit revealed by Cain's words: "Am I my brother's keeper?"

III. THE DELUGE—Chapters 5-9

1. Note how carefully family records were kept. We are not dealing with legends.

2. What do you think is the best verse in Chapter 5? Why? Cf. Hebrews 11:5 (Cf. is the abbreviation of the Latin word meaning *compare*).

3. What verse in Chapter 6 gives most pointedly the cause of the flood?

4. Why did Noah find favor in the eyes of God?

5. What do you suppose Noah's contemporaries thought of him while he was building the ark? How did he stand the test? Cf. Hebrews 11:7.

6. Consider the terrible punishment of sin in the coming of the flood.

7. Note how exact data in Chapters 7 and 8 give evidence of the historical character of this record. Some account of a great flood in the dim past has been found among practically all peoples of the earth.

8. What light does 8:20 throw on Noah?

9. Of what is the rainbow a token?

10. The ark is a type of salvation through Christ. Those people are saved who through faith enter into union with Him.

IV. LIST OF NATIONS—Chapters 10-11

1. Note again the careful family records.

2. Note the division of the earth among the descendants of the three sons of Noah. This division of the human race is recognized at this very day, namely *Semitic, Japhetic, and Hamitic.*

3. The account of the confusion of tongues at Babel in its setting of exact data gives every evidence of being a true historical record, in spite of the many attacks made upon it.

B. Patriarchal History. Chapters 12-50.

I. ABRAHAM-ISAAC—Chapters 12-27

Chapter 12

1. In the calling of Abraham we meet with the beginning of a new epoch in God's dealing with humanity. It appears that on account of religious degeneration and increasing idolatry there was danger that the knowledge of the true God might be completely lost among men. God therefore called Abraham, a God-fearing man, to take his family and remove from the idolatrous environment in which he found himself and go to the land of Canaan where he might become the progenitor of a new people, who under the special direction and blessing of God might preserve the knowledge, the worship, and the service of the true God. With God's calling of Abraham, therefore, there begins the history of Israel, the chosen people of God.

In the promise to Abraham—"in thee shall all the families of the earth be blessed"—we have a prophecy which has universally been understood as pointing to the coming of Jesus Christ as Savior, who was born of a descendant of Abraham. We have here, therefore, a continuation of the history of Redemption begun in Gen. 3:15.

As to the date of the calling of Abraham, we have no sure knowledge. Ussher places the event in the year 1921 B. C., but scholars differ in their calculations.

2. Note that Abraham is called Abram to begin with, and Sarah is known as Sarai. We shall see later how their names were changed.

3. What trait of Abram is revealed in 12:7 and 8.

4. Does Abram's conduct, 12:10-20, seem to fit the character of a chosen man of God? Strangely enough, God can use very imperfect instruments if they will but permit Him to fashion them.

Chapter 13

Compare Abram and Lot.

Chapter 14

1. What evidences are there in this chapter that it is a record of historical events rather than of legends?

2. Note again Abram's generous spirit.

3. Why did Abram refuse to take any booty?

Chapter 15

1. Note how the Lord reassures Abram in the presence of his doubts.

2. What fact is stated in v. 6? Cf. Rom. 4:1-5.

3. In v. 8 Abram asks for a sign. In accordance with God's instructions he prepares a sacrifice, but has to wait till sun-down for the sign. This comes in the form of a great darkness accompanied by God's prophecy of the sufferings of the Israelites in Egypt. These words are reinforced by the vision of the smoking furnace moving among the pieces of the sacrifice. This suggests suffering. But there is also a flaming torch which indicates hope in the midst of darkness. Finally the Lord reaffirms His promise of the land to Abram.

Chapter 16

Note how lack of faith leads to complications and difficulties.

Chapter 17

1. Here Abram and Sarai receive their new names. Abram, meaning *exalted father,* is changed to Abraham, meaning *father of a multitude* and prophetic of his position as the progenitor of a great people. In regard to the change in Sarai's name Matthew Henry offers the following comment: "*Sarai* signifies *my princess,* as if her honor were confined to one family only. *Sarah* signifies a *princess*—namely *of multitudes,* or signifying that from her should come the Messiah, the prince, even the prince of the Kings of the earth."

3. Why did God delay so long in giving Abraham and Sarah a son?

Chapter 18

1. Note the generous hospitality of Abraham and Sarah.

2. Note Sarah's difficulty in believing the Lord's words regarding a son.

3. What motivated Abraham's petitions in vs. 23-33?

NOTE REGARDING THEOPHANIES.—Several times in the Old Testament, as here, it is recorded that God appeared to men in some physical form. In His essence God cannot be apprehended by our physical senses, for "God is a Spirit" (John 4:24). But at times God has chosen to manifest Himself to our senses, as in a human form, a burning bush, or a voice that can be heard. Such manifestations, particularly if in human form, are called *the-*

ophanies, from two Greek words meaning *God* and *to appear.* It has been a favorite thought with many Bible students that when God is recorded as having appeared in human form, the manifestation was that of the Second Person of the trinity, the Son, who later became permanently incarnate in Jesus Christ.

Chapter 19
1. We have here a picture of the terribleness of sin and its consequences.
2. Why were the inhabitants of Sodom so angry with the man who came to lodge in Lot's house? See v. 9.
3. Why did Lot's wife look back?

Chapter 20
Why did Abraham practice the deceit recorded here? He has still much to learn of faith and trust in God.

Chapter 21
1. How long a time had passed from the first promise to Abraham until the birth of Isaac? Cf. 12:1-14 with 21:5.
2. Why did Hagar and Ishmael have to leave?
3. Ishmael became the founder of a numerous people, the Ishmaelites, who ultimately formed the chief element in the Arab nation.
4. For the typical significance of Ishmael and Isaac. Cf. Gal. 4:22-31.

Chapter 22
1. Why did God's command to Abraham constitute a very severe trial?
2. In what sense did Abraham sacrifice his son?
3. What did Abraham learn from this experience?

Chapter 23
1. How were Abraham and Sarah regarded by their neighbors?
2. Note how carefully Abraham provides for a burial ground as the property of his family. He did not want to be dependent on strangers.

Chapter 24
1. Why was Abraham so greatly concerned about what kind of a wife his son was to have?
2. What traits does Abraham's servant reveal?
3. What impression of Rebekah do you get?

Chapter 25
1. Form an estimate of Abraham's character.
2. Why was Esau's selling of his birthright especially wrong?

Chapter 26
Note the repetition of the Lord's promise to Isaac.

Chapter 27

How did Rebekah and Jacob suffer for their deceit?

II. JACOB–JOSEPH—Chapters 28-50

Chapter 28

1. Note that in connection with Jacob's dream God repeats the promise already given to Abraham and Isaac.
2. What do you think of Jacob's vow?
3. The word Bethel means *the house of God.*

Chapter 29

What memories do you think were called up in Jacob's mind by the deceit practiced upon him?

Chapter 30

1. Note the birth of Joseph. Who was his mother?
2. What significant statement is made by Laban in v. 27?
3. What do you think of Jacob's methods of enriching himself?

Chapter 31

1. What was the cause of the difficulty between Laban and Jacob? How was it settled?
2. How long had Jacob been in Haran?
3. Mizpah (v. 49) means *the watch tower.* Memorize the "Mizpah" greeting.

Chapter 32

1. Why did Jacob send gifts to Esau?
2. Jacob's wrestling is a symbol of prayer.
3. Note the change of Jacob's name to Israel, meaning *he who striveth with God.* Jacob had his faults, as we have seen, but God blessed him and used him when he gave God the control of his life.

Chapter 33

Note the beautiful reconciliation between the two brothers.

Chapter 34

A dark chapter—one sin leads to others.

Chapter 35

1. What creditable acts by Jacob are recorded in v. 1-7?
2. List the names of the twelve sons of Jacob.
3. Note that Esau and Jacob cooperated in the burial of Isaac.

Chapter 36

The posterity of Esau; note that he was the progenitor of the Edomite people.

Chapter 37

1. Why was Joseph hated by his brothers?
2. Was he a tell-tale?
3. Is it an undesirable thing to be a dreamer?
4. What did Joseph's brothers do to him?
5. Note that Jacob is again deceived.

Chapter 38

Another dark chapter. Sin is ugly, and the Bible in its stark realism does not gloss it over.

Chapter 39

1. What passages especially reveal Joseph's character?

2. What was the source of Joseph's power to withstand temptation?

3. How do you account for Joseph's promotions?

Chapter 40

What was the secret of Joseph's ability to interpret dreams?

Chapter 41

1. What led to Joseph's release from prison?

2. What trait of Joseph is revealed in v. 16?

3. How old was Joseph when he became prime minister of Egypt?

4. What wise measures did he suggest and carry out in connection with the famine?

Chapter 42

1. What brought Joseph's brothers to Egypt?

2. Why did he treat them as he did?

Chapter 43

Why was it so difficult for Jacob to let Benjamin go to Egypt?

Chapter 44

How was Joseph's treatment of his brothers successful?

Chapter 45

1. What traits of Joseph are revealed in this chapter?

2. Why did Paraoh make the generous offer to Joseph's family?

3. How did the report of Joseph affect his aged father?

Chapter 46

1. Note how God directed Jacob.

2. How many were the Israelites when they went to Egypt?

3. Note the meeting of Joseph and his father.

Chapter 47

1. Where were the Israelites settled?

2. Note the responsible role that Joseph plays during the famine.

3. Why was Jacob so insistent on being buried with his father?

Chapter 48

Note Jacob's blessing of Joseph's sons. We shall see later how the two tribes descending from them were given portions of land in Canaan on a par with Jacob's own sons.

Chapter 49

Note Jacob's prophecies regarding his sons and their descendants. V. 10 is regarded as a prophecy that the Messiah was to come of the Judah line.

1. Note the honorable burial that Jacob received.
2. What light do vs. 15-21 throw on Joseph?
3. What do you note in vs. 24-25?

ADDITIONAL STUDY SUGGESTIONS

In case time is not available for carrying through the study plan outlined on previous pages, the following suggestions are offered. Some of these suggestions may serve also for the purposes of review or emphasis in case the study plan has been followed.

1. Let the teacher select and assign for study only the more important suggestions offered, especially those with which notes of some length are included.

2. List the facts that are stated or may be inferred in connection with God's work of creation.

3. List all the things of which the beginning is recorded in Genesis.

4. There are two parallel lines of development running through the Old Testament: 1) the history of Israel from Abraham on, and 2) the history of Redemption through Christ. Trace these two lines as far as recorded in Genesis. For convenience in the study of the history of Redemption the following passages are listed: Gen. 3:15; 12:1-3; 26:1-5; 28:10-15; 49:10.

5. Make a study of types in Genesis. A type is a person, thing, or event in the Old Testament foreshadowing a person, thing, or event in the New Testament. (See Norlie: *The Open Bible,* pages 580-587.)

6. Make a study of the leading characters in Genesis.

7. Note the journeys of Abraham on the map, page 45.

NOTABLE PASSAGES IN GENESIS

These passages are listed for convenient reference, for special study, or for memorizing.

The Account of Creation, 1:1—2:7. The Garden of Eden, 2:8-17. The Institution of Marriage, 2:18-24. The Fall into Sin, 3. The First Gospel Promise, 3:15. Cain and Abel, 4. The Flood, 6:1—8:22. The Tower of Babel, 11:1-9. The Calling of Abraham, 12:1-5. The Rescue of Lot, 14:12-24. Abraham's Prayer for Sodom, 18:16-33. The Destruction of Sodom, 19:15-26. The Birth of Isaac, 21:1-5. The Offering Up of Isaac, 22:1-19. The Marriage of Isaac and Rebekah, 24. Jacob and Esau, 25:20-34; 27:1-46. Jacob's Dream, 28:10-22. Jacob and Rachel, 29:1-30. Birth of Joseph, 30:22-24. The Mizpah, 31:49. Jacob's Wrestling, 32:24-32. Reconciliation of Jacob and Esau, 33:1-15. The Story of Joseph, 37:1-36; 39:1—50:26.

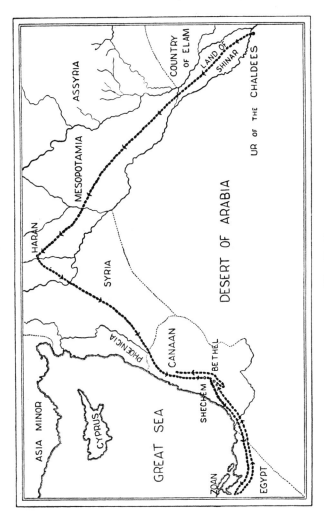

Map No. 1
Journeys of Abraham

CHAPTER X

Exodus: Deliverance from Egypt

NAME.—*Exodus* means *going out*. This book is so named because it tells of the Israelites *going out* of Egypt.

AUTHOR.—Moses.

NUMBER OF CHAPTERS.—40.

CONTENTS.—Continuing the historical account begun in Genesis, the book of Exodus tells of the deliverance of the Israelites from the bondage in Egypt, the journey to Sinai, and the experiences in the wilderness up to the time of the completion and dedication of the Tabernacle.

OUTLINE OF EXODUS

General Contents: Deliverance of Israelites from Egypt					
Historical Section—Chapters 1-19					
Bondage Chapter 1	Moses' Early Life Chapters 2-4	Ten Plagues Chapters 5-11	Pass- over Chapter 12	Deliver- ance Chapters 13-14	Journey to Sinai Chapters 15-19
Legislative Section—Chapters 20-40					
Giving of the Law Chapters 20-24		Tabernacle and Priesthood Chapters 25-31		Golden Calf Episode Chapters 32-34	Tabernacle Built and Dedicated Chapters 35-40

STUDY SUGGESTIONS

A. HISTORICAL SECTION. Chapters 1-19.

I. THE BONDAGE OF THE ISRAELITES. Chapter 1

1. What was the reason for the condition of the Israelites in Egypt?
2. What promise to Abraham had been fulfilled?

II. MOSES' EARLY LIFE. Chapters 2-4

1. How did Moses get his name?

2. What traits of Moses are revealed in 2:11-15?

3. Note the manner in which God manifested Himself to Moses (3:1-6).

4. Why is 3:8 a key verse?

5. Note in 3:14 the name by which God reveals Himself to Moses.

6. Did Moses' hesitancy show him to be a man of humility or a man lacking in courage?

7. How did God meet his objections?

III. THE TEN PLAGUES. Chapters 5-11

1. What sort of man was the Pharaoh reigning at this time? What was his first reaction to Moses' request?

2. What trial did Moses have to endure? 5:20-23.

3. How did God reassure Moses? 6:1-8.

4. List the ten plagues visited upon the Egyptians.

5. Did God harden Pharaoh's heart? When men persist in disobeying God's will, can they blame God for the consequences in deterioration of character?

IV. THE PASSOVER. Chapter 12

1. How were the Israelites saved from the tenth plague?

2. What effect did the tenth plague have on Pharaoh?

3. How many Israelites left Egypt?

4. How long had they been there?

5. Why is the Passover so called?

6. The Passover is a striking type of redemption through Christ. Note the following points:

a). *Need:* Bondage and suffering in Egypt—under sin.

b). *Origin:* In the love of God.

c). *The Means:* The slaying of a lamb without blemish and the sprinkling of blood—Christ, the sinless one, died for us.

d). *Effects:* Salvation from death, deliverance from bondage, and entrance into Canaan—Heaven.

e). *Application:* For all who believe and obey God, without reference to character or degree of faith.

7. The cleansing of the leaven from the houses in preparation for the feast of unleavened bread is a type of putting sin out of the life of the Christian.

V. DELIVERANCE. Chapters 13-14

1. What course did the Israelites take out of Egypt? Why?

2. What do you note in 13:19?

3. What do the pillars of cloud and fire symbolize? How does God show us the way today?

4. Into what difficult position did the Israelites come?

5. What did Moses do in this emergency?

6. What way out did God provide?

IV. JOURNEY TO SINAI. Chapters 15-19

1. What is the leading thought in the song of Moses? Chapter 15.

2. How were the people supplied with food and drink? 15:23—16:36.

3. Manna typifies the Word of God—the bread of life; also Christ, the bread that came down from heaven. Cf. John 6:48-51.

4. Why was the Manna given for one day at a time, except on the sixth day?

5. Getting water from the rock (17:6) typifies life from Christ. Cf. I Cor. 10:4.

6. What do you note in 17:11-12? What general truth may be derived from this episode?

7. What do you think of Jethro's advice to Moses? Chapter 18.

8. Where did the Israelites encamp in the third month after leaving Egypt? See map on page 49.

9. Note the impressive description in 19:16-25.

B. LEGISLATIVE SECTION. Chapters 20-40.

I. GIVING OF THE LAW. Chapters 20-24

1. Why is chapter 20 important? Fix in mind this chapter.

2. How do you account for the attitude of the people in 20:19?

3. Chapters 21-23 contain various ordinances and laws for the life of the Israelites, which God gave to Moses. They constitute most interesting reading.

4. Note in chapter 24 that Moses made a written record of the ordinances, called the *book of the covenant*.

5. Note also the impressive way in which the covenant was sealed.

6. What unusual experience did Moses have? 24:12-18.

II. INSTRUCTIONS ABOUT THE TABERNACLE AND THE PRIESTHOOD. Chapters 25-31

1. From whom did Moses get instructions for the construction of the Tabernacle and its furniture? Why is this fact significant? What impressions do you get from these instructions?

2. The Tabernacle and its furniture may be interpreted as types of Christ as follows:

The Tabernacle itself—Christ incarnate in the flesh.

The furniture of the outer court:

1. The brazen altar—Christ our sacrifice for sin.

2. The laver—Christ our cleanser.

The furniture of the Holy Place:

1. The table of show-bread—Christ our food.

2. The golden candlesticks—Christ our light.

3. The altar of incense—Christ our intercessor.

The furniture of the Holy of Holies:

1. The ark, containing the Law—Christ in His life fulfilling the Law.

2. The mercy-seat—Christ in His death a propitiation for sin.

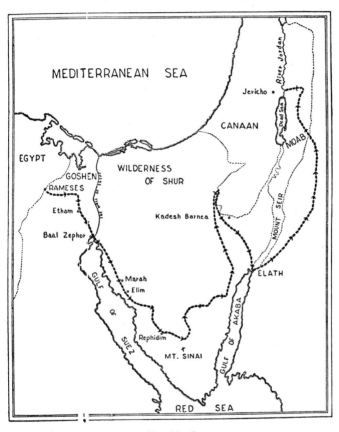

Map No. 2
Journeys of the Israelites

3. Chapters 28-29 contain divine instructions regarding the garments and consecration of the priests, Aaron, and his sons.

4. Note the inscription on the gold plate to be worn on the high priest's forehead. 28:36-38. What was its significance?

5. The priests are types of Christ.

6. What significant lesson regarding work may be derived from 31:1-11?

III. THE GOLDEN CALF EPISODE. Chapters 32-34

1. How do you account for the action of the people here?

2. Aaron's idea of making an image of a calf shows the influence of the worship of sacred animals in Egypt.

3. What do you think of Moses' conduct in 32:19-20?

4. Why were the people so severely punished? 32:25-28.

5. Note how earnestly Moses intercedes for the people (32:30-32) and how God brings the people to repentance.

6. Why did Moses' face shine when he came down from Mt. Sinai? 34:29-35. What spiritual lesson is suggested by this?

IV. THE TABERNACLE AND ITS FURNITURE BUILT AND DEDICATED. Chapters 35-40

1. How were the money and materials for the construction work obtained?

2. How generous were the people? 36:5-7.

3. Note the extreme care with which the divine instructions were followed in the construction work. 36:8—39:43. Note especially 39:42-43.

4. What facts are recorded in chapter 40?

5. How was God's approval of the work manifested? 40:34-38.

Note on the Date of the Exodus

There is considerable divergence of opinion among scholars as to the date of the Exodus. Ussher gives it as 1491 B. C. Later archaeological research indicates that this date is probably too early. Davis in his *Dictionary of the Bible* favors the date 1320 B. C., which is probably more correct.

Additional Study Suggestions

1. Trace in Exodus the developments in the history of Israel.

2. Do the same for the history of Redemption. Note the typical significance of the Passover, Tabernacle, Priesthood, sacrifices, pillar of fire or cloud, manna, and the water from the rock. Look up the passages in the Epistle to the Hebrews in which the meaning of some of these things is set forth.

3. Study the preparation of Moses for his life mission.

4. List the ten plagues and their effects.

5. Note the miraculous features connected with the departure of the Israelites from Egypt.

6. Note the circumstances connected with the giving of the written Law.

7. Note the specific instructions given by God for the construction of the Tabernacle.

8. Do the same for the setting up of the priesthood.

9. Make a study of the leading characters in Exodus.

10. Note on the map, page 49, the course of the Israelites from Egypt to Sinai.

NOTABLE PASSAGES IN EXODUS

The Birth and Childhood of Moses, 2:1-10. Moses and the Burning Bush, 3. Instructions to Moses and Aaron, 4. The Ten Plagues, 7:1—11:10. The Institution of the Passover, 12:1-28. The Deliverance from Egypt, 12:29-36. The Crossing of the Red Sea, 13:17—14:31. Moses' Song of Triumph, 15:1-19. The Miracle of the Manna, 16:1-26. The Holding up of Moses' Hands, 17:8-13. The Giving of the Ten Commandments, 20:1-17. Instructions Regarding the Tabernacle, 25:1—27:21. The Holiness Plate of the High Priests' Mitre, 28:36-38. The Golden Calf Episode, 32:1-35. The Setting Up and Dedication of the Tabernacle, 40:17-38.

CHAPTER XI

Leviticus: Laws and Regulations for the Nation

NAME.—*Leviticus* means *pertaining* to the *Levites*. The Levites were the descendants of Levi, one of the twelve sons of Jacob. To them as priests and assistants was committed the function of conducting the religious worship of the Israelites and all services connected therewith, as well as of instructing and supervising the people in morals. *Leviticus* contains in considerable detail laws and regulations for the guidance of the Levites and the people in matters of religion and morality.

AUTHOR.—Moses.

NUMBER OF CHAPTERS.—27.

OUTLINE OF LEVITICUS

General Contents: Laws and Regulations Concerning				
Sacrifices Chapters 1-7	The Priesthood Chapters 8-10	Defilement and Purification Chapters 11-22	Festivals Chapters 23-25	Obedience, Vows, Tithes Chapters 26-27

STUDY SUGGESTIONS

On account of the survey nature of these Bible study helps we shall not devote a great deal of time to Leviticus. The study of the book is certainly interesting and profitable, but the somewhat technical nature of the contents makes an extended study less essential to our purpose of getting a whole-view of the Bible. While a reading of the whole book is recommended, our specific study suggestions concern only selected portions.

Almost the entire contents of Leviticus are of a typical character pointing to Christ as substitutionary offering for sin and Redeemer of men. The sacrificial system, the priesthood, and the sacred seasons all have typical meanings. This idea should be kept constantly in mind in reading this book. It would be well also to read the Epistle to the Hebrews in this connection for the light it throws upon Old Testament institutions and rites.

I. LAWS CONCERNING SACRIFICES. Chapters 1-7.

1. By whom were these laws and regulations given?
2. Note the five sacrifices listed in 1:1—6:7. Their significance seems to have been as follows:

a). Burnt-offerings (Chapter 1)—dedication of self to God.

b). Meal-offerings (Chapter 2)—thanksgiving for spiritual blessings.

c). Peace-offerings (Chapters 3)—thanksgiving for the peace of reconciliation.

d). Sin-offerings (Chapter 4)—expiation for sin in general.

e). Trespass-offerings (Chapters 5:1—6:7)—expiation for particular sins.

II. LAWS CONCERNING THE PRIESTHOOD. Chapters 8-9.

1. Note the consecration of Aaron and his sons to the priesthood in 8:1-13. What were the chief elements in the consecration service?

2. The *Urim* and *Thummim* (8:8)—meaning *lights* and *perfections*—were stones set in the breastplate of the high priest, and apparently symbolized the divine guidance of Israel through the priests.

3. Note the episode in 10:1-7. Why were Nadab and Abihu so severely punished? Cf. Exod. 30:9.

III. LAWS CONCERNING DEFILEMENT AND PURIFICATION. Chapters 11-22.

1. List the order of events in the service on the annual Day of Atonement. Chapter 16.

2. Note the facts in regard to the two goats. First the goat of sacrifice was slain and his blood sprinkled upon the altar. Then confession of sins was made over the head of the scapegoat and he was sent away into the wilderness. This was an impressive way of emphasizing the fact that atonement precedes forgiveness. Without the shedding of blood there is no remission of sin. (Hebr. 9:22.)

IV. LAWS CONCERNING FESTIVALS. Chapters 23-25.

1. Note the seven festivals to be observed. Chapter 23.

a). The *Sabbath,* weekly, on the seventh day. 23:1-3.

b). *Passover* and *Unleavened Bread,* annually in commemoration of the deliverance from Egypt. 23:4-8. Since the death and resurrection of Jesus occurred at the time of the Passover, our Easter comes at the time of the Old Testament Passover.

c). *The Feast of First Fruits and Harvest,* an annual Festival of thanksgiving, at the beginning of the harvest season. 23:9-14.

d). *Pentecost,* an annual festival of thanksgiving at the completion of the harvest season. 23:15-22. It was at the time of this festival that the Holy Spirit was poured out upon the disciples of Christ; hence a festival under the name Pentecost was continued in the Christian Church as a commemoration of this event.

e). *The Feast of Trumpets.* 23:23-25. This festival seems to have marked the beginning of the Jewish civil year, as the Passover marked the beginning of the religious year.

f). *The Day of Atonement.* 23:26-32. This was the annual day of humiliation and prayer, the only one on which the high priest entered into the Holy of Holies. The services for the day are described in Chapter 16, as we have noted.

g). *The Feast of Tabernacles.* 23:33-44. This was a festival of eight days during which men lived in booths made of branches of trees in commemoration of God's protecting care during the wilderness wanderings.

2. What were the regulations for the Sabbatical Year? 25:1-7.

3. What were the regulations for the Year of Jubilee? 25:8-55.

NOTABLE PASSAGES IN LEVITICUS

The Day of Atonement, Chapter 16. The Sabbatical Year, 25: 1-7. The Year of Jubilee, 25:8-55.

CHAPTER XII

Numbers: The Nation in Training

NAME.—The book of *Numbers* derives its name from the fact that it records two numberings of the people of Israel, one at Mt. Sinai, and the other in Moab.

AUTHOR.—Moses.

NUMBER OF CHAPTERS.—36.

CONTENTS.—The book of *Numbers* deals in general with the experiences of the Israelites in the wilderness. Leaving Mt. Sinai, they moved on to the southern border of Canaan, where they sent spies into the country. The majority of the spies advised against trying to enter the land. Their advice was acted on by the people, and as a consequence they were condemned to wander in the wilderness for about 38 years more. At the close of the book they had arrived in the land of Moab, on the east side of the Jordan.

OUTLINE OF NUMBERS

General Contents: The Israelites in the Wilderness			
The First Census Chapter 1	Instructions for the Camp and March Chapters 2-9	Journey from Mt. Sinai to Moab via Kadesh Chapters 10-21	The Second Census and Preparations to Enter Canaan Chapters 22-36

STUDY SUGGESTIONS

I. THE FIRST CENSUS. Chapter 1.

1. List the tribes with the number of men able to bear arms in each and the total of all.

2. Which Tribe was the largest?

3. Why were not the Levites similarly numbered?

4. What were their functions as to the Tabernacle?

II. INSTRUCTIONS FOR THE CAMP AND MARCH.

Show by a diagram the plan of the encampment. Chapter 2.

III. JOURNEY FROM MT. SINAI TO MOAB VIA KADESH. Chapters 10-21.

1. How did God indicate when to break camp, where to march, and when to stop on the march? 10:11-12.

2. List the divisions in the order of march. 10:13-36.

3. Of what did the people complain? 11:4-9.

4. How did God deal with them? 11:10-35.

5. What was the cause of the rebellion of Miriam and Aaron? 12:1-3.

6. How were they punished? 12:4-15.

7. Why were the spies sent into Canaan? Chapter 13.

8. What reports did they bring back?

9. What recommendations did they make?

10. What made the difference between Joshua and Caleb and the other spies?

11. How did the people react? Chapter 14.

12. What punishment was inflicted upon them?

NOTE ON THE WANDERINGS IN THE WILDERNESS.— The Israelites clearly demonstrated by their reaction to the recommendations of the spies that they did not possess the right spirit. This can be explained partly by the fact that they had been slaves in Egypt and had had no military training equipping them for a campaign of conquest in Canaan. But the basic cause of their weakness was their lack of complete faith and trust in God. They had been given abundant reasons for such trust by the Lord's previous dealings with them, and it was their failure to believe that God could and would give them success that brought the judgment upon them. By the end of the forty years a new generation had come on the scene, trained and disciplined and possessing more perfect reliance on the guidance and power of God.

13. What was the cause of the rebellion led by Korah, Dathan, and Abiram? Chapter 16.

14. How were they punished?

15. Note the death of Miriam at Kadesh. 20:1.

16. Of what did the people complain at Meribah? 20:2-13.

17. What command did Moses receive?

18. What sin did he commit?

19. How did he suffer for it?

20. Note the death of Aaron at Mount Hor. 20:22-29.

21. How did his death affect the people?
22. Of what did the people again complain? 21:4-9.
23. How did God deal with them?
24. Of what is the brazen serpent a type? Cf. John 3:14-15.
25. Note the failure of the Amorites to withstand the Israelites. 21:21-31. This instance is typical of many other experiences recorded in this book.

IV. The Second Census and Preparations to Enter Canaan. Chapters 22-36.

1. Who was Balak? Chapter 22.
2. What request did he make of Balaam? Balaam was a Midianite, but possessed a certain knowledge of the true God.
3. Why did he not grant Balak's request to curse Israel?
4. Instead of cursing Israel, what did Balaam do? Chapters 23-24.
5. Note the Messianic prophecy in 24:17.
6. Of what sin were the Israelites guilty in connection with the Midianites? Chapter 25.
7. How was it punished?
8. How do the results of the second census compare with those of the first? Cf. 26:51 with 1:46.
9. What change in the leadership of Israel was provided for at this time? 27:12-23.
10. What tribes were settled on the east side of the Jordan? Chapter 32.

Additional Study Suggestions

1. What does Numbers contribute to our knowledge of the history of Israel?
2. What does Numbers contribute to the unfolding of the plan of Redemption? Note the judgment of the Lord upon unbelief and disobedience in the failure to occupy Canaan, the miraculous preservation in the wilderness, the episode of the brazen serpent, and the movement toward Canaan.
3. Make a study of leading characters in Numbers.
4. Note on the map, page 49, the course of the wanderings of the Israelites.

Notable Passages in Numbers

The First Census, Chapter 1. The Plan of the Encampment, Chapter 2. The Aaronic Blessing, 6:22-27. The Order of the March, 10:1-28. The Lust for Flesh, Chapter 11. The Rebellion of Miriam and Aaron, Chapter 12. The Report of the Spies, 13:1—14:10. The Rebellion of Korah, Dathan, and Abiram, 16:1-35. The Budding of Aaron's Rod, Chapter 17. Water from the Rock at Meribah, 20:1-13. The Serpent of Brass, 21:4-9. The Story of Balak and Balaam, Chapter 22-24. A Messianic Prophecy, 24:17. The Second Census, Chapter 26.

CHAPTER XIII

Deuteronomy: A Book of Reviews

NAME.—Literally *Deuteronomy* means the *second law*. This book is so called because it contains a review of the Mosaic Law.

AUTHOR.—Moses.

NUMBER OF CHAPTERS.—34.

CONTENTS.—Standing at the end of his career and facing a new generation grown up since the departure from Egypt and the first giving of the Law, Moses here surveys in a series of addresses the history of Israel, reviews and interprets the Law and the Covenant, and gives the people his farewell injunctions. This was excellent and needful preparation for the occupation and settlement of the Promised Land. The place is the plains of Moab.

OUTLINE OF DEUTERONOMY

General Contents: A Series of Reviews by Moses			
First Address: A Historical Review Chapters 1-4	Second Address: Review and Exposition of the Law Chapters 5-26	Several Addresses Dealing with the Covenant, Warnings, and Blessings Chapters 27-33	Appendix by Another Author: Vision and Death of Moses Chapter 34

STUDY SUGGESTIONS

On account of the review character of this book we shall not stop long with it. We note only a few passages.

I. THE FIRST ADDRESS: AN HISTORICAL REVIEW OF THE EXPERIENCES OF THE ISRAELITES FROM MT. SINAI TO MOAB AND EXHORTATIONS BASED THEREON. Chapters 1-4.

58

1. What were the place and circumstances of this address? 1:1-5.

2. What exhortations does Moses give in 4:1-40?

II. THE SECOND ADDRESS: AN EXTENDED EXPOSITION OF THE TEN COMMANDMENTS AND EXHORTATIONS BASED THEREON. Chapters 5-26.

1. An address of rich and varied content. Note especially Chapter 8.

III. SEVERAL ADDRESSES. Chapters 27-33.

1. What was the purpose of the monument to be erected as set forth in 27:1-8?

2. List some of the main blessings of obedience, 28:1-14, and some of the main curses that will result from disobedience. 28:15-68.

3. Note the renewal of God's covenant with Israel. 29:1-9.

4. What choices are set before the people in 30:15-20?

5. What charges does Moses give to the people, 31:1-6, and to Joshua, 31:7-8?

6. What action did Moses take in regard to the Law? 31:9-13 and 31:24-27.

7. What instructions (31:16-22) did Moses receive and obey in regard to the song in 32:1-43?

8. What are the main ideas in the song?

9. What do you note in 32:48-52?

10. Note the blessings pronounced on each of the twelve tribes. Chapter 33.

IV. THE APPENDIX. Chapter 34.

1. What vision did Moses have?

2. Where did he die and where was he buried?

3. How old did he become?

4. How did the people feel about his death?

5. Who succeeded him?

6. What was unique about Moses? Form an estimate of his character and achievements.

NOTABLE PASSAGES IN DEUTERONOMY

Passages quoted by Jesus (Matt. 4:1-11) in Resisting the Tempter, 8:3; 6:16; 6:13. The Law of Love, 6:4-5. Admonitions to Israel, Chapter 8. A Commission for Religious Education, 11:18-21. A Messianic Prophecy, 18:18. Blessings and Curses, Chapter 28. The Choice Between Life and Death, 30:15-20. Moses' Charge to Joshua, 31:1-8. The Song of Moses, 32:1-43. Death of Moses, Chapter 34.

CHAPTER XIV

Joshua: Taking Possession of the Promised Land

NAME AND AUTHORSHIP.—The Book is named from its author and principal character. The name Joshua means *Jehovah is salvation,* and later, in the Greek, appears in the form *Jesus.* Joshua was born during the bondage in Egypt and was about 54 years of age at the time of the Exodus. It will be remembered that he was one of the twelve spies sent into Canaan and that later he was consecrated by Moses as his successor in the leadership of Israel.

NUMBER OF CHAPTERS.—24.

PERIODS OF HISTORY.—At this point in our study it may be well to get a birds-eye view of the whole *history of Israel* and the historical books that record it. We may make the following divisions:

I. *The Beginnings of the Nation—from Abraham to Moses.* Recorded in the Pentateuch—*Genesis, Exodus, Leviticus, Numbers,* and *Deuteronomy.*

II. *The Confederation of Independent Tribes.* Recorded in *Joshua, Judges,* and *Ruth.*

III. *The Monarchy—Rise and Fall.* Recorded in *I and II Samuel, I and II Kings,* and *I and II Chronicles.*

IV. *The Return from Captivity.* Recorded in *Ezra, Nehemiah,* and *Esther.*

CONTENTS OF JOSHUA.—Resuming the historical account after the death of Moses the book of Joshua tells of the preparations for the conquest of Canaan, the subjugation of the various cities and districts, and the division of the lands among the tribes of Israel. The closing chapters record the farewell discourses and the death of Joshua.

OUTLINE OF JOSHUA

General Contents: Taking Possession of the Promised Land			
The Conquest Chapters 1-12	The Division of the Lands Chapters 13-21	Farewell Addresses of Joshua Chapters 22:1–24:28	Appendix by Another Author: Death of Joshua Chapter 24:29-33

STUDY SUGGESTIONS

I. THE CONQUEST. Chapters 1-12.

1. List the items in the Lord's charge to Joshua. 1:1-9.

2. What commands did Joshua issue? 1:10-15.

3. What response did the people make? 1:16-18.

4. What experiences did the two spies sent by Joshua meet with? Chapter 2.

NOTE.—Rahab, the keeper of the inn where the spies lodged, had formerly been a woman of ill-fame, but had apparently repented and reformed, to judge by her conduct at this time. Note also a passage in Hebrews (11:31), where her piety is spoken of.

5. In what state of mind did the spies find the inhabitants of Jericho? 2:8-11.

6. How did the Israelites get across the Jordan? Chapter 3.

7. What do you note in 3:7?

8. What instructions regarding memorial stones were given and carried out? Chapter 4. What was the significance of taking the stones from the river-bed?

9. What other monument did Joshua set up? 4:9-10. Why?

10. How did the report of the crossing of the Jordan affect the Canaanites? 5:1.

11. Note the resumption of the rite of circumcision which had been neglected during the wilderness wanderings. 5:2-9.

12. What do you note in 5:10-12?

13. Note Joshua's vision in 5:13-15. Many Bible students think that it was the Son of God who appeared to Joshua here. Note that in 6:2, which seems to be a part of the same vision, He is called Jehovah. The appearance with a drawn sword seems to symbolize the fact that Israel was now for a time to enter upon a military career, under the Lord's leadership.

14. Why did God provide for the fall of Jericho in such a strange way? Chapter 6.

15. What happened to Rahab?

16. What is meant by "the devoted thing?" 6:17-19.

17. What curse was pronounced upon Jericho? 6:26. Note the fulfillment in I Kings 16:34.

61

18. What was the cause of the defeat of the Israelites at the hands of the men of Ai? Chapter 7.

19. Why was Achan's sin so severely punished?

20. Why did the Israelites succeed in the second attack on Ai? Chapter 8.

21. Note the setting up of the altar and the reading of the law (8:30-35) as previously commanded by Moses. Cf. Deut. 27:1-8.

22. Note in Chapter 9 that in spite of the deceit practiced by the Gibeonites the leaders of Israel regarded as sacred and binding the covenant they had sworn to.

23. Chapters 10-12 record the continued conquest of the land. The whole period of the conquest covered about six years.

II. THE DIVISION OF THE LAND. Chapters 13-21.

1. Note on the map, page 64, the areas assigned to the various tribes. Note that the tribes of the sons of Joseph, Ephraim and Manasseh received lands on a par with the tribes of Jacob's sons.

2. In 18:1 it is told that the Tabernacle was set up at Shiloh. This then became the religious capital of Israel. Locate on map.

3. Why were the cities of refuge so called? 20:1-9. How many were there?

4. The Levites, who were the religious and moral guides and teachers of Israel, were not concentrated in any one district as were the other tribes, but were settled in 48 cities scattered throughout the lands, including the six *cities of refuge*. Note the instructions for this arrangement given by Moses in Numbers 35:1-8, and the manner in which they were carried out in Joshua 21.

5. What do you note in 21:43-45?

III. FAREWELL ADDRESSES OF JOSHUA. Chapters 22:1— 24:28.

1. Joshua delivered three farewell addresses:

a). To the two and a half tribes east of the Jordan. 22:1-8.

b). To the nine and a half tribes west of the Jordan. Chapter 23.

c). To all Israel in Shechem. 24.1-28.

In these addresses he reminded them of God's rich blessings to them and urged them to be faithful in their worship and service of the true God.

2. What choice did Joshua put before Israel? 24:14-15.

3. What decision did the people make? 24:16-24.

4. What was done to impress their decision upon their minds and hearts? 24:19-25.

IV. APPENDIX. Chapter 24:29-33.

1. This appendix by another author records mainly the death and burial of Joshua, and the burial of Joseph's remains.

ADDITIONAL STUDY SUGGESTIONS

1. What progress in the history of Israel does Joshua record?
2. What is the religious significance of the book?

3. Form an estimate of the character and achievements of Joshua.

4. Note on the map, page 64, the division of the land among the tribes of Israel.

NOTABLE PASSAGES IN JOSHUA

The Experiences of the Spies, Chapter 2. The Crossing of the Jordan, 3:14-17. The Commemorative Monument, 4:1-8. The Capture of Jericho, Chapter 6. The Sin of Achan, Chapter 7. The Capture of Ai, 8:1-29. The Deceit of the Gibeonites, Chapter 9. The Sun and Moon Standing Still, 10:12-14. The Cities of Refuge, Chapter 20. The Death of Joshua, 24:29-31. The Burial of Joseph's Bones, 24:32.

Map No. 3
The Lands of the Twelve Tribes of Israel

CHAPTER XV

Judges: A Book of Cycles

NAME.—The book derives its name from the fact that it deals with that period of the history of Israel when God raised up men called *Judges* to lead and govern the people.

AUTHOR.—The authorship of this book is uncertain. Tradition ascribes it to Samuel.

NUMBER OF CHAPTERS.—21.

CONTENTS.—The book pictures the political, social, and religious conditions of the Israelites during the period of the Judges. The people had settled down permanently in the lands which had been won from the Canaanites. Contrary to the will of God, however, the land had not been completely cleared of the Canaanites, and those who remained exerted a powerful influence upon the Israelites. The religion of the Canaanites centered around the worship of the male deity, Baal, and the female deity, Ashtoreth, and was connected with the most shameful licentious rites and sexual immoralities. To the debasing influence of this religion the Israelites were constantly exposed, and time after time they departed from the worship of the true God and turned to idolatry with its demoralizing practices. In punishment of their unfaithfulness God permitted the heathen people round about to oppress Israel until in their dire distress they would cry out for deliverance. At this time there was not a central government, as had been the case under Moses and Joshua, to which the people might turn for leadership and help in their repentant state. God, therefore, raised up emergency men, called Judges, to lead the people in victorious battle against their oppressors, set the Israelites free, and serve as their governors.

Following their deliverance the Israelites would be

faithful to God for a time, but sooner or later would again relapse into idolatry with oppression and appeal for deliverance. Over and over again the cycle is repeated—sin, oppression, repentance, deliverance, peace. To abstain from idolatry with its accompanying evils was evidently a difficult course to pursue.

The Judges combined the offices of military leaders and civil magistrates. The jurisdiction of some of them probably extended over only a part of the country, and some of them may have been contemporaries. The office was not hereditary.

The following is a list of Judges mentioned by name, together with the tribe of each, and the oppressing enemies.

JUDGES OF ISRAEL

JUDGES	TRIBE	ENEMY
1. Othniel	Judah	Mesopotamians
2. Ehud	Benjamin	Moabites
3. Shamgar	Judah (?)	Philistines
4. { Deborah	Ephraim	Canaanites
{ Barak	Naphtali	....
5. Gideon	W. Manasseh	Midianites
6. Abimelech	W. Manasseh	....
7. Tola	Issachar	....
8. Jair	E. Manasseh	....
9. Jephthah	Gad	Ammonites
10. Ibzan	Zebulun (?)	....
11. Elon	Zebulun	....
12. Abdon	Ephraim (?)	....
13. Eli	Levi	Philistines
14. Samson	Dan	Philistines
15. Samuel	Levi	Philistines

OUTLINE OF JUDGES

General Contents: Israel under the Judges		
Preface: The Need of the Judges Chapters 1-2	The Work of the Judges Seven Cycles of Apostasy, Oppression, and Deliverance Chapters 3-16	Stories of Micah and the Levite Chapters 17-21

STUDY SUGGESTIONS

I. PREFACE. THE SITUATION IN GENERAL SHOWING THE NEED OF THE JUDGES. Chapters 1-2.

1. Note in 1:1 that some of the Canaanites were still in the land.

2. What recurring expression is found in verses 27 to 33 in chapter 1?

3. What judgment of the Lord is set forth in 2:1-5?

4. What general picture is presented in 2:11-23?

II. THE WORK OF THE JUDGES. Chapters 3-16. In this section are described seven cycles of apostasy, oppression, and deliverance.

We note only a few of them.

1. Note the concise account of the first cycle. 3:7-11.

2. Note in chapter 4 the account of the work of a woman Judge, Deborah. With her was associated Barak in the judgeship. A song commemorating their victory over the oppressors is recorded in chapter 5.

3. Who is the oppressor in the cycle described in chapter 6?

4. Who is raised up as deliverer?

5. What sign did the angel give? 6:19-24.

6. What significant act of Gideon is described in 6:25-32?

7. What reassuring signs did Gideon ask and receive? 6:36-40.

8. Why was Gideon's army reduced? 7:1-8.

9. Why was the test described in 7:4-7 an effective means of selection?

10. What do you think of Gideon's strategy? 7:15-23.

11. The story of the Judge Samson, of giant strength, is recorded in chapters 13-16. What was the cause of Samson's downfall? Chapter 16.

III. STORIES OF MICAH AND THE LEVITE. Chapters 17-21.

These stories serve as illustrations of the religious and moral degeneration that took place in this period of the history of Israel.

ADDITIONAL STUDY SUGGESTIONS

1. Show the political and religious significance of the Book of Judges.

2. What cycle reoccurs?

3. Make a study of some of the better known Judges.

4. How were the Judges types of Christ?

NOTABLE PASSAGES IN JUDGES

General Statement about the Judges, 2:14-19. The First Cycle, 3:7-11. The Story of a Woman Judge, Chapter 4. A Song of Triumph, Chapter 5. The Story of Gideon, 6:7—8:32. Jephthah and His Daughter, Chapter 11. The Story of Samson, Chapters 13-16.

CHAPTER XVI

Ruth: A Beautiful Idyl

NAME.—The name is derived from the chief character in the book.

AUTHOR.—Probably Samuel.

NUMBER OF CHAPTERS.—4.

CONTENTS.—This little book tells the story of how Ruth, a woman of the Gentile people, the Moabites, became a member of Israel and an ancestress of David, and thus of Jesus Christ. The event took place during the period of the Judges, and is in beautiful contrast to the rough and immoral life prevailing among many of the Israelites at this time.

OUTLINE OF RUTH

Ruth's Return with Naomi from Moab Chapter 1	Ruth Favored by Boaz Chapter 2	Ruth's Engagement to Boaz Chapter 3	Ruth's Marriage to Boaz Chapter 4

STUDY SUGGESTIONS

1. Read the book at one sitting.
2. What were the reasons for Naomi's going to and returning from Moab? 1:1-6.
3. What were the names of Naomi's husband, sons, and daughters-in-law?
4. What traits of character does Ruth reveal? 1:7-18.
5. What type of man was Boaz? Chapter 2.
6. Why was Ruth favored by Boaz?
7. What was Naomi's motive in her instructions to Ruth? 3:1-5.

NOTE.—There was a law in Israel that if a man died childless, it was the duty of a near kinsman to purchase his inheritance and to marry his widow. Boaz was a kinsman of Ruth's deceased husband, Mahlon, and was willing to assume these responsibilities. But there was

68

another man nearer of kin than Boaz. According to the law this kinsman was entitled to the first chance to redeem the inheritance, but he did not care to avail himself of the opportunity. Hence Boaz had the responsibilities legally and publicly transferred to himself and married Ruth. These facts are set forth in the remainder of the story.

8. Note that Ruth became the mother of Obed who became the grandfather of David. 4:17. She thus came into the royal line of the Messiah. This line came down from Judah through his son, Pharez, as set forth in the genealogy in 4:18-22. Jesus therefore, through Ruth, was partially of Gentile blood.

9. Why was Ruth rewarded as she was?

ADDITIONAL STUDY SUGGESTIONS

1. What bearing does the Book of Ruth have upon the development of the plan of redemption?

2. Characterize each of the leading persons in the story.

NOTABLE PASSAGES IN RUTH

Ruth's Declaration of Faithfulness, 1:16-17. The Kindness of Boaz, 2:1-17. Ruth's Place in the Messiah Line, 4:13-17.

CHAPTER XVII

I Samuel: The Beginning of the Monarchy

NAME.—This book derives its name from the fact that *Samuel* is the most important character in the book, especially in the first part.

AUTHOR.—The authorship of this book is not known. Samuel, Nathan, Gad, and David may have written parts of it.

NUMBER OF CHAPTERS.—31.

CONTENTS.—This book records the life and judgeship of Samuel, his heroic efforts to stem the tide of national degeneration, the request of the people for a king, the appointment, reign, rejection, and death of Saul.

OUTLINE OF I SAMUEL

General Contents: Beginning of the Monarchy						
Career of Samuel		Career of Saul				
His Preparation Chapters 1-3	His Work Chapters 4-7	His Appointment Chapters 8-10	His Reign Chapters 11-14	His Rejection Chapters 15-16	His Persecution of David Chapters 16-27	His Death Chapters 28-31

STUDY SUGGESTIONS

I. SAMUEL'S PREPARATION. Chapters 1-3.

1. What were the circumstances of Samuel's birth? Chapter 1. *Samuel* means *asked of God.*

2. What do you note in 1:11? According to Hannah's vow Samuel was to be consecrated to God as a Nazirite. Such a dedication might be for life or for a limited period. In Samuel's case it was to be for life. According to Hebrew usage a Nazirite must

abstain from the use of wine or strong drink, cutting the hair, **and** touching a dead body. He was to be wholly dedicated to God.

3. What is told about the sons of Eli in 2:12-17?

4. What effort did Eli make to remedy conditions? 2:22-25.

5. What prophecy is uttered in 2:27-36?

6. Note the beautiful story of God speaking to Samuel. Chapter 3. Why do you think God chose Samuel as a mouthpiece for speaking to Eli? What was the gist of the message?

7. What do you understand 3:1b to mean?

8. What is said of Samuel in 3:19-21?

II. SAMUEL'S WORK. Chapters 4-7.

1. What disasters overtook the Israelites as recorded in Chapter 4?

2. What effects accompanied the presence of the ark among the Philistines? Chapter 5. What did they finally do with it? Chapter 6.

3. What reformation did Samuel bring about? 7:3-6.

4. What divine intervention in favor of Israel is recorded in 7:7-11?

5. What was the significance of the monument set up by Samuel? 7:12. *Ebenezer* means the *stone of help.*

6. What office did Samuel hold? 7:15-17.

III. SAUL'S APPOINTMENT AS KING. Chapters 8-10.

1. What condition is described in 8:1-3?

2. What request did the people bring to Samuel? 8:4-5.

3. What was Samuel's reaction to the request? 8:6.

4. What guidance did he get from God? 8:7-18.

5. How do you account for the persistency of the people in their attitude? 8:19-22.

NOTE ON THE ESTABLISHMENT OF THE MONARCHY.— By God's law the form of government among Israel up to this time had been a Theocracy. That is, a government in which men lived under the immediate direction of God. This form could have continued had the people been united in a vital faith in Him and in obedience to His guidance. But they failed to live up to this high expectation. They forsook God and worshipped idols, disobeyed God's clear injunctions, and engaged in shamefully sinful practices. As a consequence the nation was fast degenerating both in its civic and religious life. The people saw that the nations round about them were ruled by kings and they hankered after the glamor of a royal establishment among themselves. They wanted to be like their heathen neighbors in this respect. The more serious among them thought, too, that their nation would be strengthened by centralization of government under a visible king who might lead them both in peace and war. The wickedness of Samuel's sons as judges brought matters to a head. And so the elders of the people called an assembly to present their formal demand for a king to the aged Samuel. He hesitated at first and by the Lord's guidance presented a dark picture of what they would have to endure under a king. The people, however, persisted in their demand, and by the guidance of God Samuel granted their request by the selection and annointing of Saul as their first king.

The date of the establishment of the monarchy was probably about 1050 B. C.

6. What impression of Saul do you get from 9:1-2?

7. What circumstances caused Saul to visit Samuel? 9:3-14.

8. How was Samuel guided in the selection of Saul? 9:15-17.

9. Note the courteous manner in which Samuel treated Saul who was to displace him in the government of the people. 9:18-24. What light does this throw upon Samuel's character?

10. How did Samuel make known to Saul that he was to be king? 9:25—10:1.

11. What ability of Samuel is revealed in 10:2-8?

12. What new experiences of Saul are recorded in 10:9-13?

NOTE ON THE SCHOOLS OF THE PROPHETS.—We meet here for the first time reference to the institution generally known as the *Schools of the Prophets*. These schools were a kind of theological seminary of training for the prophetic office. They were apparently instituted by Samuel as agencies in the religious reformation of the people which he undertook. The course of study included the Law and its interpretation, sacred music, and poetry. The prophetic gift was an endowment of the Holy Spirit by virtue of which the possessor was able in a special degree to know, understand, and proclaim the will of God. Usually, but not always, it included the ability to predict future events. According to the above passage Saul received the prophetic gift.

13. Note that Saul is publicly proclaimed king at Mizpah. 10:17-27.

IV. Saul's Reign. Chapters 11-14.

1. What light is thrown upon the character of Saul in Chapter 11?
2. Note the general public recognition of Saul as king. 11:12-15.
3. Since Israel now had a king, Samuel brings his judgeship to a close and admonishes the people to be faithful to God, as recorded in chapter 12. What claim does he make in 12:1-5?
4. How old was Saul when he began to reign? 13:1.
5. Chapters 13 and 14 record successful wars with the Philistines.
6. Of what wrong-doing was Saul guilty and what judgment upon him was pronounced by Samuel? 13:8-14.
7. What military successes of Saul are recorded in 14:47-48?

V. Saul's Rejection. Chapters 15-16.

1. What sin on the part of Saul caused his rejection by God? Chapter 15.
2. How did Samuel feel about Saul's failure? Note especially 15:35.
3. What action did Samuel take at God's direction? 16:1-13.
4. What significant fact about Saul is recorded in 16:14?
5. What did David do for him? 16:15-23.

VI. Saul's Persecution of David. Chapters 17-27.

1. What remarkable deed by David is recorded in chapter 17?
2. Why did David reject Saul's armor? 17:38-40.
3. What was the secret of David's success? 17:41-49.
4. What devoted friendship is recorded in 18:1-4?
5. What was the cause of Saul's enmity to David? 18:5-9.
6. What efforts did he make to get rid of David? 18:10-29.
7. Chapters 19 to 26 record the almost constant persecution of David by Saul. At least seven times David narrowly escaped death. He was forced to flee time after time and hide in caves. Jonathan befriended him and tried to bring about a reconciliation between Saul and David but without success. Saul's failure, the departure of the Lord's Spirit from him, and the influence of the evil spirit made him jealous, morose, and vindictive. David, on the other hand, although hunted like a wild animal, maintained a generous attitude toward Saul and twice spared his life when Saul was in his power. One of these incidents is recorded in chapter 24 and throws much light on the characters of the two men.
8. Note the death of Samuel. 25:1. He may be regarded as a type of Christ.

VII. The Death of Saul. Chapters 28-31.

1. In what difficult situation did Saul find himself? 28:3-6.
2. What did he do in his distress? 28:7-14.

3. What message was brought to him by the spirit of Samuel? 28:15-19.

4. How did it affect Saul? 28:20-25.

5. How did Saul die? 31:1-6.

6. Note how shamefully the Philistines treated his body and how the Israelites rescued and buried it. 31:7-13.

7. What thoughts are suggested by the career of Saul?

ADDITIONAL STUDY SUGGESTIONS

1. Point out the political and religious significance of I Samuel.
2. Make a study of the character and career of Samuel.
3. Do the same for Saul.

NOTABLE PASSAGES IN I SAMUEL

The Birth of Samuel, Chapter 1. The Call of Samuel, Chapter 3. The Loss of the Ark, 4:1-18. The Request for a King, Chapter 8. The Anointing of Saul to Be King, 10:1. Saul's Disobedience and Rejection, 13:1-14. The Anointing of David, 16:1-13. David and Goliath, Chapter 17. The Friendship between David and Jonathan, 18:1-4. The Jealousy of Saul, 18:5-11. David Spares Saul's Life, Chapter 24. Saul Consulting the Witch of Endor, Chapter 28. The Death of Saul, Chapter 31.

CHAPTER XVIII

II Samuel: The Monarchy at Its Height

NAME.—*I and II Samuel* were originally one book called the *Book of Samuel.* When, later, the book was divided, the name II Samuel was retained for the second part even though the death of Samuel is recorded in the first part.

AUTHOR.—Unknown. Possibly Nathan and Gad, two contemporaries of David, who is the chief character in the book.

CONTENTS.—This book records the reign of King David, first over the tribe of Judah, for seven years, and then over all the Israelites, for 33 years. Among other events the book records the centralization of civil and religious government in Jerusalem, the extension of the kingdom from Egypt to the Euphrates River, the fall and restoration of David.

OUTLINE OF II SAMUEL

General Contents: The Reign of King David				
David King over Judah Chapters 1-4	David King over all Israel Chapters 5-10	David's Fall Chapters 11-18	David's Restoration Chapters 19-20	Various Records Chapters 21-24

STUDY SUGGESTIONS

I. DAVID KING OVER JUDAH. Chapters 1-4.

1. What report was brought to David by the Amalekite? 1:1-12. It is not clear whether this story told to David is true or not. If true, it is a more detailed account of the death of Saul than that recorded in I Samuel 31. Whether true or false the Amalekite expected favors from David for bringing him this report of the death of his enemy Saul. In this he was sadly mistaken, however, as is shown by David's order to have him slain. 1:13-16. That

David was generous-hearted and grieved rather than rejoiced over the fate of Saul is evidenced by the hymn of lamentation which he composed. 1:17-27. In this song David's sorrow over Saul is mingled with profound grief over the death of his beloved friend, Jonathan.

2. What trait of David is revealed in 2:1?

3. What fact is stated in 2:4?

4. Chapters 2-4 record incidents of civil war between the followers of Saul and the followers of David and the ultimate victory of David's house. David, however, consistently showed respect to the house of Saul. This is evidenced in particular by his displeasure over the slaying of Saul's general, Abner, by his own general, Joab, and by the punishment visited upon the slayers of Saul's son, Ishbosheth. 4:5-12.

II. David King over All Israel. Chapters 5-10.

1. What facts are recorded in 5:1-5?

2. What place was made the capital of the kingdom? 5:6-12.

3. What disposition was made of the Ark? Chapter 6.

4. What intention of David is recorded in 7:1-3?

5. Did this intention meet with God's favor? 7:4-17. God had other work for David to do than that of building a temple. He was to extend and consolidate the kingdom. God reserved for his son and successor, Solomon, the task of building the temple, a work for which he was better fitted than David.

6. What promise was given to David as to the permanency of his dynasty? 7:12-16. This was fulfilled in Christ, born of the Davidic line.

7. What light is thrown upon David's character by his treatment of Mephibosheth, Jonathan's son and Saul's grandson? Chapter 9.

8. Other portions of this section, Chapters 5-10, record David's success in overcoming the traditional enemies of Israel and in largely extending the kingdom.

III. David's Fall. Chapters 11-18.

1. Of what grievous sins was David guilty as recorded in chapter 11?

2. How was he brought to a realization of the enormity of his sins? 12:1-14.

3. How was he punished? 12:15-23.

4. In addition to the sorrow caused by the death of his child, David suffered greatly because of domestic difficulties including the bold rebellion of his son Absalom which eventuated in Absalom's tragic death. These matters are recorded in chapters 13-18.

IV. David's Restoration. Chapters 19-20.

These chapters record chiefly the return of David to Jerusalem, following the failure of Absalom's rebellion, and the quelling of an insurrection led by Sheba.

V. THE LAST DIVISION OF THIS BOOK.

Chapters 21-24 contain an account of certain victories over Philistine giants, songs of praise and prophecy by David, lists of military heroes, and punishment for a census taken contrary to the will of God.

ADDITIONAL STUDY SUGGESTIONS

1. What contribution did David make politically?

2. In considering the religious significance of II Samuel, note the promise to David of perpetuity for his line. 7:12-16. Cf. Matt. 9:27 and Matt. 21:9.

3. Consider David as a type of Christ both in humiliation and exaltation. Cf. Psalm 22:1 with Matt. 27:46. See also Ezekiel 34:23.

4. Form an estimate of the character and achievements of David.

5. Note on the map, page 78, the extent of the kingdom of David.

NOTABLE PASSAGES IN II SAMUEL

David's Lament over Saul and Jonathan, 1:17-27. David Made King over Judah, 2:1-4. David Made King over all Israel, 5:1-5. Making Jerusalem the Capital, 5:6-10. The Ark Brought to Jerusalem, Chapter 6. David and Bethsheba, 11:1—12:24. The Revolt of Absalom, Chapters 15-18.

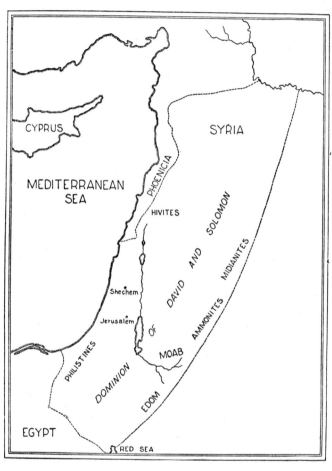

Map No. 4
Dominion of David and Solomon

CHAPTER XIX

I Kings: The Disruption of the Monarchy

NAME.—I and II Kings were originally one book. They are so called because they deal with the records of the kings of Judah and Israel.

AUTHOR.—Unknown. I and II Kings are a compilation from various sources of which the following are mentioned: *Acts of Solomon, Book of the Chronicles of the Kings of Judah,* and *Book of the Chronicles of the Kings of Israel.* The compiler may have been Jeremiah who lived towards the end of the period covered in II Kings. Evidences indicate that the source books were written by contemporaries.

CONTENTS.—The book records the crowning of David's son, Solomon, as king, the greatness of his reign, the construction of the Temple, growing idolatry and corruption, the division of the kingdom into Judah and Israel, and the subsequent history of the two kingdoms for about eighty years.

OUTLINE OF I KINGS

General Contents: The Disruption of the Monarchy		
Reign of Solomon	Division of the Kingdom	History of Judah and Israel
Chapters 1-11	Chapter 12	Chapters 13-22

STUDY SUGGESTIONS

I. THE REIGN OF KING SOLOMON. Chapters 1-11.

1. What plot is recorded in 1:1-11?
2. How was the plot frustrated? 1:12-53.
3. What charge did David give to Solomon? 2:1-4.
4. How long did David reign? 2:11.
5. Who succeeded him? 2:12.
6. The balance of Chap. 12 records the execution of Solomon's brother, Adonijah, and other political enemies.

7. What fact is recorded in 3:1? This was clearly a diplomatic marriage and suggests the foreign policy adopted by Solomon, which was that of forming friendly alliances with neighboring countries and dealing with them by diplomacy rather than by force of arms.

8. What gift did Solomon ask and receive from God? 3:4-15.

9. What proof of his wisdom did he give? 3:16-28.

10. What evidences of the extent, magnificence, and splendor of Solomon's reign are recorded in 4:20-34?

11. What was the purpose of the treaty made with Hiram, the King of Tyre? Chapter 5.

12. When did Solomon begin the erection of the Temple? 6:1.

13. How long did it take to complete it? 6:37-38.

14. How did the Temple compare in size with the Tabernacle? 6:2. (In cubit measurement the Tabernacle was 10x10x30.)

15. What total impression of the Temple do you get? Chapter 6.

NOTE ON TEMPLES. There were three different Temples built in Jerusalem.

1) *The Temple of Solomon* was begun probably in 967 B. C. and was destroyed by Nebuchadnezzar in 587 B. C. This Temple was the most glorious and costly building of antiquity. The value of the materials of which it was built was enormous.

2) *The Temple of Zerubbabel,* built after the return from the Babylonian exile, was begun probably in 537 B. C. and taken down by King Herod in 19 B. C. This was much less splendid than the first Temple.

3) *The Temple of Herod* was begun in 19 B. C. and destroyed at the time of the fall of Jerusalem in 70 A. D. This was much more splendid than the second Temple, though not as glorious as the first.

16. When the Temple and its furniture had been completed, a high festival of dedication was held. In solemn procession the Ark was brought from the Tabernacle and placed in the Holy of Holies in the Temple, and vast sacrifices were offered. The approval of God was shown by a cloud of glory which filled the Temple. Solomon delivered an address reviewing the circumstances and purposes of the building of the Temple, offered a beautiful prayer of dedication, and closed with an admonition to the people to be faithful in their worship of Jehovah. Chapter 8.

17. In addition to the Temple, Solomon built an elaborate place for himself (7:1-12) and one for his wife, the daughter of Pharaoh (9:24).

18. What interesting episode is recorded in 10:1-13?

19. What impression of the material magnificence of Solomon's reign do you get from the record in 10:14-29?

20. Of what sins did Solomon become guilty? 11:1-8.

21. What judgment upon him was pronounced by God? 11:9-13.

22. By raising up one adversary after the other God sought to bring Solomon to repentance, but apparently in vain, and his reign ended in disorder and gloom.

23. How long did Solomon reign? 11:41-42.

II. THE DIVISION OF THE KINGDOM. Chapter 12.

1. What proposition did the people present to Rehoboam? 12:1-5.

2. What conflicting advice did he receive? 12:6-11.

3. What advice did he follow? 12:12-15.

4. What was the result? 12:16-20.

5. What did Rehoboam attempt to do? 12:21-24.

6. Why did he desist?

7. How did Jeroboam attempt to consolidate and strengthen his kingdom? 12:25-33.

NOTE ON THE DIVISION OF THE KINGDOM

The causes of the division among the Israelites were deep-seated and some of them of long standing. The other tribes became keenly jealous of the large and increasingly dominating role played by the tribe of Judah, in whose territory Jerusalem, the capital, was located. Added to this, Solomon's policy of foreign alliances weakened national ties; intermarriage with heathen peoples and idolatry loosened the binding power of the true religion upon the people as a whole; and the heavy taxes and forced labor necessary to sustain Solomon's enormous and luxurious establishment nurtured a spirit of discontent and revolt. A crisis was reached when Rehoboam refused to grant the request of the people for relief and reform. Ten tribes, all but Judah and Benjamin, immediately revolted and chose Jeroboam as king. The capital of this seceding kingdom was established in Shechem, (later in Samaria), and in order to wean the people away from Jerusalem and all it stood for, rival centers with idolatrous worship were set up at Bethel and Dan. The two tribe kingdom, which remained true to the house of David and continued the Messianic line, is known as the Kingdom of Judah, or the Southern Kingdom. The ten tribe kingdom is spoken of as the Kingdom of Israel, or the Northern Kingdom.

The division of the kingdom took place probably in 931 B. C.

III. SUBSEQUENT HISTORY OF JUDAH AND ISRAEL. Chapters 13-22.

The relationship between the two kingdoms was generally one of hostility. At times, however, they combined against a common foe. During the reigns of David and Solomon several of the surrounding nations had been subjugated by the Israelites, but by the disruption of the kingdom these vassal states were encouraged to revolt and regain their independence. Furthermore, the fabulous wealth and splendor of Jerusalem enticed expeditions of plunder into the land of Israel. The country was therefore in a state of almost constant warfare.

Idolatry was steadily on the increase in both kingdoms, but especially in Israel. In the Kingdom of Judah some degree of true religion was always preserved.

In order to call the people to repentance and guide them in periods of special difficulty God raised up a noble line of prophets who did not hesitate to proclaim the whole will of God whether for comfort or for chastisement.

Some kings made earnest efforts to maintain true religion and righteous government, but most of them were swept along by the prevailing tide of idolatry and were guilty of injustice and misrule.

The most wicked king of all was Ahab, King in Israel. Influenced by his heathen wife, Jezebel, daughter of the King of Sidon, he aggressively promoted the debasing worship of Baal and Ashtoreth. He was repeatedly warned and admonished by the valiant prophet Elijah whose character and career may serve as an illustration of the role played by the prophets during this period.

1. Read the arresting story of Elijah in chapters 17-19.
2. What prediction did Elijah make? 17:1.
3. How was he provided for? 17:2-16.
4. What miracle did he perform? 17:17-24.
5. What were the effects of the drought? 18:1-6.
6. What was Ahab's attitude toward Elijah? 18:7-15.
7. Describe the trial on Mt. Carmel. 18:16-40. What thoughts are suggested by this episode?
8. How was the drought broken? 18:41-46.

9. What trials did Elijah have to endure? 19:1-8.
10. What revelations did he receive? 19:9-18.
11. Who was designated as his successor? 19:19-21.
12. What light is thrown upon the characters of Ahab and Jezebel by the episode in 21:1-16?
13. What judgment was pronounced upon them? 21:17-29.
14. How did they die? See 22:29-40 and II Kings 9:30-37.

ADDITIONAL STUDY SUGGESTIONS

1. Show the political and religious significance of I Kings.
2. Elijah is a type of John the Baptist. See Malachi 4:5-6; Luke 1:17; and Matt. 11:14.
3. Form an estimate of the character and career of Solomon.
4. Note on the map, page 84, the areas of the two kingdoms.

NOTABLE PASSAGES IN I KINGS

The Death of David, 2:1-11. Solomon's Wisdom, 3:5-28. The Magnificence of His Reign, 4:20-34. The League with King Hiram of Tyre, Chapter 5. The Dedication of Solomon's Temple, Chapter 8. Visit of the Queen of Sheba, 10:1-13. Solomon's Riches, 10:14-29. Judgment upon Solomon, 11:1-13. The Division of the Kingdom, 12:1-20. Elijah and the Widow of Zarephtah, Chapter 17. The Trial on Mount Carmel, Chapter 18. The Still, Small Voice, Chapter 19. Naboth's Vineyard, 21:1-24.

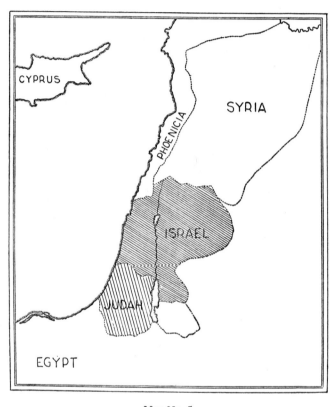

Map No. 5
The Areas of the Two Kingdoms

84

CHAPTER XX

II Kings: The Passing of the Two Kingdoms

FOR NAME AND AUTHOR—See notes on I Kings.

CONTENTS. II Kings continues the account of the subsequent history of the two kingdoms until they are completely subjugated by surrounding nations and the people are carried away into captivity.

OUTLINE OF II KINGS

General Contents: History of the Two Kingdoms	
Judah and Israel until the Fall of Israel Chapters 1-17	Judah Alone until Its Fall Chapters 18-25

For survey and reference purposes it may be useful to set down at this point certain facts about the period of the Monarchy in the history of Israel.

I. The monarchy as a unit lasted for 120 years. It had three kings each reigning 40 years, as follows:

Saul,
David,
Solomon.

II. After the disruption of the monarchy, probably in 931 B. C., the Kingdom of Israel lasted for 209 years, until 722 B. C. It had 19 kings (and one interregnum) of nine dynasties; the average length of reign was about 10 years; and all the kings were of wicked character. The brevity of the reigning periods and the frequent change of dynasties indicate the fact that this kingdom was in a state of almost constant civil war, a punishment for unfaithfulness to God.

III. The Kingdom of Judah lasted for 344 years, from 931 B. C. to 587 B. C., 135 years longer than Israel.

It had 19 kings and one queen all of the same dynasty, the house of David, the average length of reign being about 17 years. The much greater stability of this kingdom was due to a larger degree of faithfulness to true religion. Several of the kings of Judah, notably Jehoshaphat, Joash, Uzziah, Hezekiah, and Josiah were godly men and put forth earnest efforts to reform the evil conditions brought about by idolatry and other sins. The list of kings and length of reigns of the two kingdoms is as follows:

KINGDOM OF ISRAEL

Jeroboam I	Jehoahaz
Nadab	Joash
Baasha	Jeroboam II
Elah	(Interregnum)
Zimri	Zachariah
Omri	Shallum
Ahab	Menahem
Ahaziah	Pekahiah
Jehoram	Pekah
Jehu	Hoshea

KINGDOM OF JUDAH

Rehoboam	Jotham
Abijam	Ahaz
Asa	Hezekiah
Jehoshaphat	Manasseh
Jehoram	Amon
Ahaziah	Josiah
Athaliah (Queen)	Jehoahaz
Joash	Jehoiakim
Amaziah	Jehoiakin
Uzziah (or Azaria)	Zedekiah

IV. The prophets continued their valiant efforts to stem the tide of corruption, sometimes with a measure of success. The wicked kings, however, looked upon the prophets proclaiming the will of God as their enemies and opponents and greatly hindered their work, even putting many of them to death. The fact that the kingdoms did not come to an end sooner than they did was due to the gracious patience of God and the reforming activities of the prophets. In no way did it seem possible, however, to prevent the final doom of the kingdoms.

V. Large numbers of the people in the Kingdom of Israel, which came to an end in 722 B. C., were carried away into captivity by Shalmanezer, king of Assyria, and never returned. Much speculation has been engaged in as to what became of the so-called "ten lost tribes." In all probability they gradually merged with the peoples among whom they lived. In place of the removed Israelites the king of Assyria sent in heathen peoples who mingled with the Israelites still remaining in the land, thus producing a mixed people both as to race and religion. These Samaritans were never recognized as kinsfolk by the people of Judah, and hostility between them continued even to Christ's time. People of the Kingdom of Judah, which fell in 587 B. C., were taken into captivity by Nebuchadnezzar, king of Babylonia, and were permitted to return after 70 years. The continuance of Judah was of course especially significant, for it was the Messiah line.

STUDY SUGGESTIONS

Our plan permits but a brief stay with II Kings.

1. What request did Elisha make of Elijah? 2:1-10.

2. How did Elijah's life come to an end? 2:11-18.

3. What acts of Elisha are recorded in 4:1-37?

4. Note the cure of Naaman by Elisha. 5:1-19.

5. In what respects is Naaman's cure typical of salvation through Christ?

6. The fall of Israel is recorded in 17:1-6. What facts are there stated?

7. Note the fearful catalog of sins charged against Israel. 17:7-18.

8. What efforts at reformation in Judah were made by King Hezekiah? 18:1-8.

9. Note the reassuring words of Isaiah in his proclamation to Hezekiah. 19:20-34. What was the source of his strength?

10. What happened to the besieging army of the Assyrians and their king, Sennacherib? 19:35-37.

11. The final destruction of Judah is recorded in 25:1-21. What facts are there stated?

Notable Passages in II Kings

The Translation of Elijah, 2:1-15. Miracles of Elisha, Chapter 3. The Healing of Naaman, 5:1-27. The Fall of Samaria, 17:1-18. The Reformation under Hezekiah, 18:1-8. The Deliverance from Sennacherib, Chapter 19. The Fall of Judah, 25:1-21.

CHAPTER XXI

I and II Chronicles: A Survey of the Religious History of Israel

NAME.—These books were originally one in the Hebrew Canon and were called *The Acts* or *Annals of the Days*. From this title our name *Chronicles* is derived.

AUTHOR.—Probably compiled by Ezra. Numerous sources are cited in the books.

NUMBER OF CHAPTERS.—I Chronicles, 29; II Chronicles, 36.

CONTENTS.—Up to Chronicles the books of the Old Testament have been continuous, carrying the history forward step by step from the Creation to the Babylonian Captivity. In Chronicles, however, we have a brief parallel survey of these same periods. The reason that this parallel record is included in the Bible seems to be that it presents the history from a definitely religious point of view, as distinguished from the other books which view events more from a political angle. In other words, "the previous books present matters as man sees them, while Chronicles sets them forth as God sees them." As evidence of this difference may be especially pointed to the fact that Chronicles devote a large amount of space to the necessity, the conception, and construction of the Temple, that these books tell only the story of the Kingdom of Judah (the Messiah line) after the disruption of the Monarchy, and record extensively the religious reformations under Asa, Jehoshaphat, Joash, Hezekiah, and Josiah.

Additional reasons for materials in the books of Chronicles may be found in the situation obtaining after the return from the Babylonian captivity. The reassignment of lands among the returned exiles required a careful checking up of titles by means of genealogical backgrounds. Hence we find in I Chronicles detailed genealogical tables. Then, too, impetus for the rebuilding of the Temple would be given by recounting the history and significance of the former Temple such as we find in these books. Moreover, the urge to reestablishment of the religious worship required emphasis on the genealogy, hereditary functions, and prerogatives of the Levites as set forth in I Chronicles.

The chief interest in the books of Chronicles, then, may be said to be the spiritual history of Israel as the chosen people of God to whom were given the wonderful promises, in whom was preserved the knowledge of the true God in spite of all apostasies, and from whom was eventually to come the Messiah for the blessing of the nations. In addition to the more spiritual emphasis the books also contain some new material supplementing the accounts in the other historical books.

OUTLINE OF I CHRONICLES

The Records: From Adam to David	
The Genealogies Adam to David Chapters 1-10	Reign of King David: Preparations for the Temple Chapters 11-29

OUTLINE OF II CHRONICLES

The Records: Solomon to the Captivity	
Reign of King Solomon: Construction and Dedication of the Temple Chapters 1-9	History of Judah: Apostasies, Reformations, and Fall Chapters 10-36

STUDY SUGGESTIONS

Since these books, to a considerable extent, cover ground already surveyed in the previous historical books, a separate study is not imperative for our present purposes. The fuller account of the Temple and reformations, however, will richly repay study. Note especially the finding of the lost book of the Law and its effects, in the reign of King Josiah. Chap. 34.

Notable Passages in Chronicles

Preparations for Building the Temple, 1 Chron. 21. Construction and Dedication of the Temple, 2 Chron. 2-7. Reformations—under Asa, 2 Chron. 14-16; under Jehoshaphat, 2 Chron. 17-20; under Joash, 2 Chron. 24; under Hezekiah, 2 Chron. 29-33; under Josiah, 2 Chron. 34-35.

CHAPTER XXII

Ezra: Return from Captivity and Restoration

NAME AND AUTHORSHIP.—This book bears the name
of its author, Ezra, who is also one of the chief characters
in the book. Ezra was of a priestly family and was re-
nowned for his high scholarship in the field of the Sacred
Scriptures. He was possessed of a deep passion to revive
study of the Word of God and inaugurated a movement
for learning and doing the will of God of which we are
beneficiaries even to this day. Ezra is credited with the
authorship of Psalm 119, which is a poem of 22 sections
exalting the excellencies of the Law of God. Ezra led the
second group of exiles returning to Jerusalem from Babylonia.

NUMBER OF CHAPTERS.—10.

CONTENTS.—The book of Ezra records the return to
Jerusalem of about 50,000 Jews, from exile in Babylonia,
under the leadership of Zerubbabel, the rebuilding of the
Temple, the later return of about 2,000 exiles under Ezra,
and the reformation instituted by him. The book is written from a priestly, or ecclesiastical point of view.

OUTLINE OF EZRA

General Contents: Return from Captivity and Restoration			
Return under Zerubbabel Chapter 1-2	Rebuilding of the Temple Chapters 3-6	Return under Ezra Chapters 7-8	Reformation under Ezra Chapters 9-10

STUDY SUGGESTIONS

I. THE RETURN UNDER ZERUBBABEL. Chapters 1-2.

1. What items are included in the proclamation of King Cyrus?
1:1-4.

2. Zerubbabel was a prince of the house of Judah.

3. What valuables did the exiles take back with them? 1:5-11.

4. How many were there in the first group that returned? 2:64-67.

NOTE ON CYRUS.—As the founder of the great Persian empire Cyrus stands out as one of the great men of the East. Among many distinguished exploits was his conquering of the Babylonian empire, which held the people of Judah in captivity. One of the first acts of Cyrus was to permit the exiles to return to Jerusalem. Not only that —he also made provision for the rebuilding of the Temple. He thus became an instrumentality in the hands of Jehovah, whose authority he recognized, even though he was a gentile king.

II. THE REBUILDING OF THE TEMPLE. Chapters 3-6.

1. What facts do you note in connection with the laying of the foundation of the new Temple? 3:8-13.

2. What offer of cooperation in the building did Zerubbabel and his associates receive? 4:1-2. The people who made this offer were Samaritans.

3. Why was their offer rejected? 4:3.

4. What were the consequences of the rejection of the offer? 4:4-23.

5. What prophets encouraged the Jews to resume the building? 5:1-2.

6. How was the opposition finally overcome? 5:3—6:15.

7. How was the dedication of the Temple celebrated? 6:16-22.

NOTE ON THE DATES OF THE CAPTIVITY.—There are various methods by which the dates of the captivity have been computed. The one most commonly accepted is that which places the beginning at the fall of Jerusalem, in 587 B. C., and the close with the completion of the second Temple, 70 years later, about 517 B. C.

III. THE RETURN UNDER EZRA. Chapters 7-8.

By permission of Artaxerxes, King of Persia, Ezra was permitted to lead another division of about 2,000 exiles in return to Jerusalem. This was about 60 years after the completion of the Temple.

IV. THE REFORMATION UNDER EZRA. Chapters 9-10.

Ezra found a sad state of moral and spiritual degeneration among the people in and about Jerusalem. The chief fault was intermarriages with the heathen neighbors with the consequent apostasy. Ezra boldly and earnestly called upon the people to repent and put away their heathen spouses. He was largely successful, and the true worship was restored.

Note Ezra's impassioned confession and prayer in 9:5-15.

ADDITIONAL STUDY SUGGESTIONS

1. Point out the political and religious significance of the book of Ezra.

2. Form an estimate of the character and career of Ezra.

NOTABLE PASSAGES IN EZRA

The Proclamation of Cyrus, 1:1-4. The Returning Exiles, 2:64-67. Beginning the Rebuilding of the Temple, 3:8-13. Completion and Dedication of the Second Temple, 6:13-22. Ezra's Confession and Prayer, Chapter 9.

CHAPTER XXIII

Nehemiah: Restoration and Reformations

NAME AND AUTHORSHIP.—This book, too, bears the name of its chief character, Nehemiah, who was also, most probably, the author of the book. In fact the book is largely autobiographical in character. Nehemiah means *The Lord comforts us*. He was of the tribe of Judah, born in exile, and had risen to the high position of cup-bearer to Artaxerxes, King of Persia, before he became governor at Jerusalem. He was a man of deep piety and patriotism and possessed great strength of purpose and qualities of leadership.

NUMBER OF CHAPTERS.—13.

CONTENTS.—The book records the appointment by King Artaxerxes of Nehemiah as governor at Jerusalem, the rebuilding of the city walls in the face of bitter opposition, religious and social reforms. Nehemiah begins at a point in time about 12 years after the last events recorded in Ezra.

OUTLINE OF NEHEMIAH

General Contents: Restoration and Reformations		
Appointment and Arrival of Nehemiah as Governor Chapters 1-2	Rebuilding the Walls of Jerusalem Chapters 3-7	Various Reforms Chapters 8-13

STUDY SUGGESTIONS

I. APPOINTMENT AND ARRIVAL OF NEHEMIAH AS GOVERNOR. Chapters 1-2.

1. Where was Nehemiah when this book opens? 1:1.
2. What did he learn about his fellow countrymen in Jerusalem? 1:2-3.

3. How did the report affect him? 1:4-11.
4. What light does this throw upon his character?
5. What did he seek and receive from King Artaxerxes? 2:1-8.
6. What experience did he meet with on the way to Jerusalem? 2:9-10.
7. What was one of the first things he did in Jerusalem? 2:11-16.
8. What order did he issue? 2:17-19.
9. How do you account for the attitude of Sanballet and his associates? 2:19-20.

NOTE ON SANBALLET.—A Gentile of the Moabite people Sanballet filled apparently some civil or military office under Artaxerxes. Jealous of his position and fearful of the rise of the Jews under Nehemiah he did everything in his power to hinder the fortifying of Jerusalem. The apparently diplomatic marriage of his daughter to a grandson of the Jewish high priest, Eliashib, served also to embarrass Nehemiah by creating a party spirit among the Jews themselves.

His associate in opposition, Tobiah, was also connected by marriage with Jewish families, a further cause of division among the Jews. 6:17-19.

II. REBUILDING THE WALLS OF JERUSALEM. Chapters 3-7.

1. Chapter 3 tells about the various groups engaged in the work of reconstruction and the part built by each. A very fine spirit of cooperation evidently prevailed.
2. What opposition did they meet with? 4:7-12.
3. What protective measures did Nehemiah institute? 4:13-23.
4. What economic evils were reported and corrected? Chapter 5.
5. What repeated efforts were made by Sanballet and his associates to defeat Nehemiah's purposes? 6:1-14.
6. In spite of all opposition the walls of the city were completed in the surprisingly short period of 52 days, a fact which profoundly impressed the enemies and forced them to recognize the hand of God in it all. 6:15-16.

III. VARIOUS REFORMS. Chapters 8-13.

1. What significant event is recorded in 8:1-8?
2. How did the hearing of the Law of Moses affect the people? 8:9-12.
3. As a result of the reviewing of the Law the Jews, under the direction of their leaders, were moved to renew the Covenant and institute various reforms of evils that had become prevalent among them, such as neglect of the Lord's ordinances, failure to

give tithes, breaking of the Sabbath, and intermarriages with the Gentiles. These matters are recorded in Chapters 8-13.

Additional Notes on Ezra and Nehemiah

The return of the Jews to Jerusalem, the rebuilding of the Temple and the city walls, the resumption of religious services, and the carrying out of religious reforms are all tokens of the blessing of God upon the Jews as a chosen people with a distinct destiny in spite of their many failures. Through this returned remnant the knowledge of the true God was to be preserved and the Messianic idea carried to fruition.

Notable Passages in Nehemiah

The Concern of Nehemiah for His People, Chapter 1. His Permission to Return, 2:1-8. The Completion of the Walls of Jerusalem in Spite of All Opposition, Chapter 6. The Reading of the Law, Chapter 8. Nehemiah's Reforms, Chapter 13.

CHAPTER XXIV

Esther: God's Providential Care of His People

NAME.—The book is named from its principal character. *Esther* is a Persian word and means *The Star of the East*.

AUTHOR.—Probably Mordecai, Esther's uncle.

NUMBER OF CHAPTERS.—10.

CONTENTS.—This book tells the story of a Jewish girl, Esther, who became queen of Perisia, frustrated a plot of a high official, Haman, to destroy all her people in Persia, and delivered them out of the hands of their enemies. In commemoration of this deliverance the Jews observed the festival of *Purim,* so called from the circumstance that Haman had cast lots (pur) to determine on what day his massacre of the Jews was to be carried out. By the turn of events this day became instead the day of the Jews' deliverance.

A rather remarkable feature of this book is that the name of God is not mentioned in it. One explanation among others that has been offered for this is that the contents of this book may have been incorporated into the official records of the Persian Court and therefore the name of Jehovah omitted, since he was not recognized by the Persians. However, even if the name of God is not mentioned, His hand is in evidence throughout. In fact, the book of Esther was regarded by the Jews as a particularly impressive evidence of God's providential care of them as His chosen people during their dispersion, and this book was placed second only to the Pentateuch in their regard. The story is gripping in its dramatic and emotional qualities. It is also very valuable for the realistic picture it gives of life and customs at the Persian court.

General Contents: God's Providential Care of His People				
Selection of Esther to Be Queen Chapters 1-2	Haman's Plot to Destroy the Jews Chapter 3	Esther's Appeal to the King Chapters 4-5	Haman's Downfall Chapters 6-7	Deliverance of the Jews Chapters 8-10

STUDY SUGGESTIONS

1. The story moves along with such swift movement that its first reading should not be interrupted by questions. Read it through at one sitting.
2. Sketch the story in outline.
3. Note thoughts that the events in the story suggest.

NOTABLE PASSAGES IN ESTHER

Queen Vashti's Refusal to Attend Banquet, Chapter 1. Esther Chosen to Be Queen, 2:15-20. Haman's Plot, Chapter 3. Mordecai's Appeal to Esther to Intercede for Her People, Chapter 4. Haman Hanged on His Own Gallows, 7:7-10.

NOTE ON HISTORICAL BOOKS.—Esther is the last book classified among the historical books in the Old Testament. Review at this point the historical periods and books noted in connection with the study of Joshua, page 60.

CHAPTER XXV

The Poetical Books

While there is much poetry in other books of the Old Testament, the following five are usually grouped in a class by themselves as the Poetical Books: *Job, Psalms, Proverbs, Ecclesiastes, Song of Solomon.*

Hebrew poetry may be thought of in three forms: 1). Lyrical, which occupies the foremost place, 2). Gnomic, or reflective, such as the Proverbs, and 3). Dramatic, to which class, according to some scholars, Job and the Song of Solomon belong.

The poetry of the Hebrews is marked not by rhyme but by parallelism. This may be defined as "the correspondence of one verse or line with another." In the main three types of parallelism are met with—*synonymous, antithetic,* and *synthetic.*

1. SYNONYMOUS PARALLELISM is that in which the second line repeats essentially the sense of the first line in different but equivalent terms.

The following may serve as examples.
"The heavens declare the glory of God;
And the firmament showeth his handywork."

(Psalm 19:1).

"Bless Jehovah, O my soul;
And all that is within me, bless his holy name."

(Psalm 103:1).

"Oh give thanks unto Jehovah; for he is good;
For his lovingkindness endureth for ever."

(Psalm 118:1).

2. ANTITHETIC PARALLELISM is the type in which the second line presents a contrast or opposition to the first.

Examples:

"The fear of Jehovah is the beginning of knowledge;
But the foolish despise wisdom and instruction."
(Prov. 1:7).

"A wise son maketh a glad father;
But a foolish son is the heaviness of his mother."
(Prov. 10:1).

"A soft answer turneth away wrath;
But a grievous word stirreth up anger."
(Prov. 15:1).

3. SYNTHETIC OR CONSTRUCTIVE PARALLELISM is that in which there is a similarity of construction between lines, noun answering to noun, verb to verb, etc., without necessarily presenting an equivalence or contrast in sense.

Examples:

"The law of Jehovah is perfect, restoring the soul:
The testimony of Jehovah is sure, making wise the simple.
The precepts of Jehovah are right, rejoicing the heart:
The commandment of Jehovah is pure, enlightening the eyes.
The fear of Jehovah is clean, enduring forever:
The ordinances of Jehovah are true, and righteous all together." (Psalm 19:7-9).

In addition to the above types of parallelism there are other construction forms that are not easy to describe or classify. Sometimes a thought structure consists of three, four, or more lines. Throughout, however, one senses a certain rhythm of thought or construction which pleases the mind or ear with the beauty of its movement.

WISDOM LITERATURE.—Three of the poetical books, *Job, Proverbs,* and *Ecclesiastes,* belong to the *Wisdom Literature* of the Hebrews.

The *Wisdom Literature* is the nearest approach to philosophical writings in the Old Testament. Among other problems dealt with are "the moral government of the world and the duty of men in such a world." The "wise men," distinct from the priests and the prophets, were thoughtful students of life and gave utterance to many profound ideas of universal interest and significance.

CHAPTER XXVI

Job: The Problem of Suffering

NAME.—The book bears the name of its chief character, Job.

AUTHOR.—It is not known who the author of this book is. Various men have been suggested, such as Moses, Solomon, Elihu, or Job himself.

TIME OF WRITING.—This also is hidden in obscurity. Because of lack of reference to Jewish history or the Law many scholars think the book belongs in the Patriarchal period, even before the time of Moses. In that event Job would be the oldest book in the Bible. Other authorities place it very late.

NUMBER OF CHAPTERS.—42.

CONTENTS.—Job is a didactic poem, in form resembling a drama. The book deals with the profound problem of the meaning of suffering in the case of godly people. The book opens with a description of Job as a prosperous and pious man. In a scene in Heaven Satan contends that Job is pious because of what he gets for it. In other words, his piety is motivated by self interest. God gives Satan freedom to afflict Job to test him. This he proceeds to do by robbing him of his children, possessions, and health. Job is deeply grieved and perplexed, but for a time bears it all with remarkable patience. However, after seven days and nights of silent suffering in the presence of three friends, Job's patience seems to be exhausted. He complains of his lot bitterly and curses the day he was born. His three friends, adherents of the philosophy that all suffering is caused directly by sins, begin to argue with Job that he must be a hypocrite, guilty of some great hidden sin, since so great suffering has come to him. Job repels this idea and the major part of the book is occupied with arguments for and against this theory of suffering, no agreement being reached. A young relative of Job, by name Elihu, who has been sitting by in silence, now speaks up, charges Job with self righteousness and his three friends with failure to establish their accusation against Job. He then presents his own theory that suffering at times is not visited on men as chastisement for wrong-doing but as a means of testing and discipline.

Finally, God is represented as speaking to Job out of the whirlwind and by setting forth the greatness and wonder of His creation, providence, and government shows Job how ignorantly and foolishly he has acted in charging God with injustice. Job is thoroughly humbled and brought to sincere repentance. The three friends of Job are also rebuked for their error in their interpretation of Job's suffering and offer a sacrifice of repentance. Job is restored to a position greater even than before.

It may be said that Job did not receive a theoretical solution of the problem of suffering, but he was given a working solution in this that by acknowledging the unsearchable wisdom, power, justice, and glory of God he came into a relationship with God in which he could have implicit faith and trust in Him even in situations which he could not rationally comprehend.

In the opinion of competent judges the book of Job is one of the greatest in all literature. Tennyson spoke of it as "the greatest poem, whether of ancient or modern literature." And this is Carlyle's evaluation: "I call that [Job] one of the grandest things ever written with pen."

OUTLINE OF JOB

Theme: The Problem of the Suffering of the Godly					
Prologue: Job's Character and Position Chapter 1:1-5	Job's Afflictions Chapters 1:6—2:13	Arguments of Job and Three Friends Chapters 3-31	Speech of Elihu Chapters 32-37	God's Speaking and Job's Repentance Chapters 38—42:9	Epilogue: Job's Restoration Chapter 42:10-17

STUDY SUGGESTIONS

I. PROLOGUE: JOB'S CHARACTER AND POSITION. Chapter 1:1-5.

List the facts stated about Job in this section.

II. JOB'S AFFLICTIONS. Chapters 1:6—2:13.

1. What motive did Satan claim actuated Job in serving God? Chapters 6-11.
2. What permission was given Satan? 6:12.
3. How was Job afflicted? 1:13—2:10.
4. How did he bear his afflictions?
5. What three friends came to comfort him? 2:11-13.

III. ARGUMENTS OF JOB AND HIS THREE FRIENDS. Chapters 3-31.

1. What change seems to have come over Job? Chapter 3.
2. What is the gist of his complaint? Chapter 3.
3. In the speeches that follow, the friends of Job, governed by the view that all suffering is directly due to sins on the part of the sufferer, contend that Job must be guilty of great sins, accuse him of hypocrisy, and call upon him again and again to repent. Job stoutly affirms his integrity, shows that often the godly suffer and the wicked prosper, and he says some hard things about the injustice of God. They fail to reach any agreement.

IV. SPEECH OF ELIHU. Chapters 32-37.

As a young man, Elihu has hitherto refrained from speaking in the presence of his elders. But when the friends of Job have exhausted their arguments without success, and Job continues to assert his innocence, Elihu can restrain himself no longer. In a speech marked by great intensity of feeling he charges Job with presumptuousness and self-righteousness and the friends with lack of understanding in their failure to find a solution of the problem before them. He then presents his own idea that God who is unsearchable in His greatness and justice uses the ministry of suffering for the purpose of chastening and discipline. No reply is made to his speech.

V. GOD'S SPEAKING AND JOB'S REPENTANCE. Chapters 38-42:9.

1. Read thoughtfully this entire section. This is poetry of the most sublime character.
2. Of what does God accuse Job by His question in 38:2?
3. What general idea runs through Chapters 38 and 39?
4. What effect do God's challenges have upon Job? 40:3-5.
5. With what further challenges does God confront Job in Chapters 40 and 41?

6. What is the final effect on Job? 42:1-6.
7. What demand of God was conformed to by the three friends? 42:7-9.

VI. Epilogue: Job's Restoration. Chapter 42:10-17.

1. In what did Job's restoration consist?
2. The great age which Job attained is regarded as evidence that he lived in the patriarchal period.

Notable Passages in Job

The Prologue, Chapters 1-2. Job's Curse, Chapter 3. Job's Remark Regarding His Friends' Wisdom, 12:2. The Redeemer Prophecy, 19:25-26. The Voice of God, Chapters 38-41. Job's Repentance, 40:3-5; 42:1-6. Job's Restoration, 42:7-17.

CHAPTER XXVII

Psalms: Songs of Instruction, Prayer, Praise, and Thanksgiving

AUTHORSHIP.—The book of Psalms is sometimes spoken of as the Psalms of David, conveying the impression that David is the author of them all. Such is not the case, however. David is the author of only about half of them, namely 73 of the 150 Psalms. The rest are credited as follows: Asaph, 12; the Sons of Korah, 10; Solomon, 2; Moses, 1; Ezra, 1; Heman, 1; Ethan, 1; anonymous, 49. Asaph was a leader of David's choir; the Sons of Korah were singers in the Temple; Heman and Ethan were among the wise men of the time of David and Solomon.

TIME OF WRITING.—The book of Psalms represents a collection gathered over a period of about 1000 years, from the time of Moses to the Captivity.

CONTENTS.—The Psalms are of the most varied content. They contain instruction about God, creation, nature, the Messiah, the future. They represent the many varieties and manifestations of the moral and spiritual life, and experiences of the Hebrews. "The Psalter is a marvelous record of human hearts pouring themselves out from age to age in communion with God." While there are expressions of painful suffering and complaints of dire distress in the Psalms, the dominant note throughout is that of praise and thanksgiving. Some of them are fervent prayers cast in poetic form. Many Psalms were set to music and sung in the Temple services.

A writer has offered this comparison: "The law showed what religion *ought to be;* the prophets tell us very plainly what the religion of their times *was not;* the Psalms indicate what religion *was to some.*"

Something of the precious meaning which the Psalms have had for Christians throughout the centuries is clothed in expressive language by the words written by C. H. Spurgeon when he had completed his commentary on them: "A tinge of sadness is on my spirit as I quit 'The Treasury of David', never to find on this earth a richer storehouse, though the whole palace of Revelation is open to me. Blessed have been the days spent in meditating, mourning, hoping, believing, and exulting with David. Can I hope to spend hours more joyous on this side of the golden gate? The book of Psalms instructs us in the use of wings as well as words: It sets us both mounting and singing."

From ancient times the Psalms have been grouped into five divisions or books. Each closes with a doxology. The reason for the groupings has been a constant problem for Bible scholars. Among many explanations is an ancient Jewish statement that the five groupings were made to correspond to the five books of the Pentateuch. While this is an interesting theory, it is probably more fanciful than real.

The groupings of the Psalms are as follows:

Book I	Book II	Book III	Book IV	Book V
1-41	42-72	73-89	90-106	107-150

STUDY SUGGESTIONS

In the very nature of the case no adequate study of the book of Psalms can be attempted in this survey course. The Psalms constitute material for life-long study, meditation, instruction, and inspiration. All we shall attempt to do at the present time is to call attention to some matters of interest in connection with certain Psalms which are favorites with many Christians.

Psalm 1. A very clear-cut distinction between the righteous and the wicked.

Psalm 2. A prophetic Messianic psalm—Cf. Acts 4:25.

Psalm 8. The comparative insignificance yet dignity of man.

Psalm 19. A marvelous description of the works and the words of God.

Psalm 22. Quoted by Christ on the cross.

Psalm 23. The precious shepherd psalm.

Psalm 24. The King of glory.

Psalm 25. A devout prayer for pardon and guidance.

Psalm 27. A psalm of fearless trust.

Psalm 30. Thanksgiving for deliverance.

Psalm 32. A truly gospel psalm.

Psalm 42. A psalm of spiritual thirst.

Psalm 43. "Send out thy light."

Psalm 46. The inspiration for Luther's battle hymn, "A Mighty Fortress Is Our God."

Psalm 48. The beauty and glory of Zion.

Psalm 51. From the depths of a penitent heart.

Psalm 67. All the nations called upon to praise God.

Psalm 72. A psalm of world-wide missionary sweep.

Psalm 84. A glorification of the house of God. Often used at dedication of churches.

Psalm 86. A beautifully trusting prayer.

Psalm 90. Moses' psalm about the eternity of God and the brevity of man's life. Often used at funeral services.

Psalm 91. Assurances of God's care of His children.

Psalm 98. Music in praise of God.

Psalm 100. Let all men praise God.

Psalm 103. Perhaps the most beloved psalm of praise.

Psalm 104. A poetic glorification of the creative and providential work of God.

Psalm 111. The goodness of God.

Psalm 115. Heathen ideals contrasted with God.

Psalm 118. An exquisite thanksgiving psalm.

Psalm 119. The longest psalm in the Bible—a section of eight verses for each letter of the Hebrew alphabet. It is a psalm in glorification of the Word of God. N. B., v. 9.

Psalm 121. Looking upward.

Psalm 122. Prayer for the peace of Jerusalem.

Psalm 125. The safety of God's people.

Psalm 130. "Out of the depths," a prayer often used at funeral services.

Psalm 139. God is everywhere and knows all things.

Psalm 145. A psalm for Thanksgiving Day.

Psalm 150. Praise, praise, praise.

The Messianic idea is directly suggested in Psalms 2, 110, 118; indirectly in Psalms 16, 22, 40, 45, 68, 69, and 72.

Every Christian should be able to identify at least ten psalms by number and first line or other mark of identification.

CHAPTER XXVIII

Proverbs: Applied Religion

AUTHORSHIP.—As in the case of the Psalms, the book of Proverbs is also a collection gathered together over a period of time. The chief collector was Solomon who is also author of most of them. In I Kings 4:32, it is stated that Solomon spoke 3000 proverbs. Out of this large number he selected those embodied in this book in Chapters 1:1 to 22:16. The section 22:17 to 24:34 is by different authors. In Chapters 25 to 29 is another group of Solomonic proverbs collected under the auspices of King Hezekiah. In Chapter 30 are proverbs by Agur, a teacher, and in Chapter 31 are some by King Lemuel, of Arabia.

TIME OF WRITING.—As indicated above most of the Proverbs are by Solomon. The final arrangement dates probably from the time of Hezekiah.

NUMBER OF CHAPTERS.—31.

CONTENTS.—As previously stated the book of Proverbs belongs to the *Wisdom Literature* of the Hebrews. The Proverbs are trenchant statements of practical wisdom and applied religion summarizing the keen observations of the wise men, of whom Solomon was the greatest. Truth and falsehood are often personified as two women, *Wisdom* and *Folly*. Wisdom speaks words of "understanding, knowledge, prudence, subtlety, instruction, and discretion." While from Folly come words of "simplicity, brutishness, stupidity, ignorance and villainy."

The central idea of the book of Proverbs is pointedly stated in 1:7: "The fear of Jehovah is the beginning of knowledge; But the foolish despise wisdom and instruction."

It should be borne in mind that *wisdom,* among the Hebrews, included *piety* as well as *knowledge.* The wise man was the religious man, for with him religion entered into every department and activity of life. The wise men conceived of God as being present in every event. There was no cleavage between the secular and the religious. Their religion, in other words, was practically applied to life.

OUTLINE OF PROVERBS

Theme: *Applied Religion*				
Poems by Solomon in Praise of Wisdom Chapters 1-9	Proverbs by Solomon on Virtues and Vices Chapters 10:1–22:16	Proverbs by Various Authors on Many Subjects Chapters 22:17–24:34	Hezekiah's Collection of Solomon's Proverbs Chapters 25-29	Proverbs by Several Authors Chapters 30-31

STUDY SUGGESTIONS

I. POEMS BY SOLOMON IN PRAISE OF WISDOM. Chapters 1-9.

1. This portion of the book consists of connected discourses in poetic form in praise of wisdom. This is clearly indicated by the paragraph divisions in the American Standard Revised Version. In the Authorized Version there are also paragraph markings, as for instance at verses 7, 10, 20, and 24 in Chapter 1. In Moulton's *Modern Reader's Bible* the distinction among the poems is further accentuated by helpful titles supplied by the editor.

2. The first verse in Chapter 1 gives the authorship of this first division.

3. Verses 2 to 6 seem to set forth the purposes of the collection. What are some of the purposes mentioned?

4. Verse 7 sets a theme for the whole book as suggested above.

5. Verses 8-19 is the first poem in praise of wisdom. What is its central idea?

6. The next poem extends through the remainder of Chapter 1. Who is represented as speaking? What is the central idea of the message?

7. Chapter 2 constitutes another unit. What are some of the fruits of the pursuit of wisdom?

8. Formulate a title for the section 3:1-12.

9. The division, 3:13-26, contains some of the most beautiful poetry in the book. What is the main idea?

10. What practical applications of religion are made in 3:27-35?

11. The rest of the wisdom poems in this section will richly reward study. The study suggestions above merely call attention to samplings.

II. Proverbs by Solomon on Virtues and Vices. Chapters 10:1—22:16.

In this division we find 374 detached, two-line proverbs on a great many subjects. There is no common topic. Most of the ideas can, however, be grouped under the general head of virtues and vices.

III. Proverbs by Various Authors on Many Subjects. Chapters 22:17—24:34.

The Proverbs in this section are of miscellaneous character both as to form and content.

IV. Hezekiah's Collection of Solomon's Proverbs. Chapters 25-29.

This group contains mostly two-line proverbs, though there are some of greater length. The content is varied.

V. The Last Division, Chapters 30-31, consists of a series of wisdom poems by Agur, Lemuel, and probably others.

Notable Passages in Proverbs

Among the many hundred striking sayings in this book it is very difficult to make a selection. The following are perhaps among those best known: 1:7; 1:10; 3:5-6; 3:7-10; 3:11-12; 3:13-20; 4:1-9; 4:23; 6:6-11; 8:1-36; 9:10; 13:15; 14:34; 15:1; 21:27; 22:1; 22:6; 23:26; 23:29-35; 24:30-34; 31:10-31.

CHAPTER XXIX

Ecclesiastes: The Futility of Life Without God

NAME.—Ecclesiastes is the Greek rendering of the Hebrew name of this book, *Koheleth*, which means *the Preacher.*

AUTHORSHIP AND DATE.—Solomon himself is regarded by some scholars as the author of this book, according to 1:1. By others, however, another unknown author, living perhaps during the Persian ascendancy, is thought to have written the book, but to have put his words in Solomon's mouth. The problem is obscure.

CONTENTS.—The most varied differences of opinion exist among scholars as to the plan and purpose of this book. No extensive analysis will be entered upon here. The most apparent interpretation and probably the most true one is that the author has found that nothing earthly can satisfy the deepest cravings of the soul and that worldly wisdom is incapable of solving the problems of life. All of these things impress him as vain and futile. "All is vanity." There is, however, meaning to life, provided we find the true philosophy. And what this is appears clearly from the closing words of the book: "Let us hear the conclusion of the whole matter: fear God, and keep his commandments; for this is the whole duty of man. For God will bring every work into judgment, with every hidden thing, whether it be good or whether it be evil."

OUTLINE OF ECCLESIASTES

Theme: The Futility of Life Without God			
Theme: "All is vanity." Chapter 1:1-11	Disappointing Experience with Earthly Pursuits Chapters 1:12—2:26	Worldly Wisdom and Its Shortcomings Chapters 3:1—11:8	Conclusion: God must be Given the Proper Place in Life. Chapters 11:9—12:14

STUDY SUGGESTIONS

I. The Theme: "All is Vanity." Chapter 1:1-11.

1. Note the source of the ideas in the book as stated in 1:1.
2. What is the dominant note in the introductory passage 1:2-11?

II. Disappointing Experiences with Earthly Pursuits. Chapters 1:12—2:26.

In this section the preacher records his experiments with the seeking of knowledge, pleasure, possessions, and labor—all without finding any permanent satisfactions for the soul.

III. Worldly Wisdom and Its Shortcomings. Chapters 3:1—11:8.

This division deals with a wide range of observations on life and things. Worldly maxims are set forth, the best that human wisdom can suggest. These give a degree of satisfaction, but, in the final analysis, no real solution of the problems of life in such a world as human beings inhabit.

IV. The Conclusion: God Must be Given the Proper Place in Life. Chapters 11:9—12:14.

1. After the rather dismal survey offered throughout the book appears at the end a beam of light. Note the expressions: "rejoice," "Let thy heart cheer thee," "remove sorrow from thy heart" (11:9-10). But the ground on which these injunctions to happiness are based is regard for the judgments of God (11:9). Therefore the clear-cut admonition to youth: "Remember now thy creator in the days of thy youth, before the evil days come and the years draw nigh, when thou shalt say, I have no pleasure in them" (12:1). Therefore, also, the concluding verses (12:13-14), as noted above.

2. Chapter 12 is one of the best known portions of the Bible. Read it meditatively, bearing in mind that the key to the understanding of it is given in v. 1.

Notable Passages in Ecclesiastes

All Is Vanity, 1:2-11. A Time for All Things, 3:1-8. Bread Upon the Waters, 11:1. Right Rejoicing, 11:9-10. "The Conclusion of the Whole Matter," Chapter 12.

CHAPTER XXX

The Song of Solomon: A Song of Love

Author.—Solomon.

Contents.—Bible scholars vary greatly in their ideas about this book. The most common view holds that the Song portrays the love between the bridegroom, Solomon, and his bride, and that this relationship figuratively represents the love between Christ and His church.

The Song is cast in lyrical dramatic form and is of great poetic beauty especially in the passages descriptive of nature.

The reader should carefully observe the paragraph divisions as they usually represent a change in the person speaking.

On account of the nature of this Song no attempt is made at any formal outline. For largest appreciation it should be read through as a unit with a mind open to the total impression of the whole.

Notable Passages

The Rose of Sharon, 2:1-4. A Poem About Spring, 2:10-13. The Shepherd, 2:16-17. The Strength of Love, 8:6-7.

CHAPTER XXXI

The Prophetical Books

The *prophets* played a large role in the life of Israel. Their importance was so great that the history of Israel simply cannot be adequately set forth without some account of the prophets, their work and influence.

The name *prophet* is from a Greek rendering of the original Hebrew *Nabi,* and means *an interpreter of the will of God.* A prophet was one who by the special illumination of God was able, in a unique sense, to know, understand, and proclaim the will of God. Usually the prophetic gift included the ability to foretell the future, but not always.

In a wide sense the name prophet is applied to such men as Abraham, Moses, Samuel, and David, who most assuredly were interpreters of the will of God. But in a more restricted sense the term designates men belonging to the *order of the prophets* which arose at the time of Samuel and continued in an apparently unbroken line until after the return from the Babylonian captivity.

The rise of the prophetic order was apparently due to the failure of the regular Levitical priesthood to teach and guide the people adequately in matters of religion and morals. Called of God the prophets came forth to rebuke the people for their idolatry and worldliness and urge them to repent of their sins, turn back to God and the true faith, and live in harmony with the will of God. Frequently they would predict that most terrible disasters would overtake Israel if they continued in their evil ways. At times, too, they were privileged to proclaim the forgiving grace of God to those whom chastisement and suffering had made humble and penitent.

The prophets also interested themselves in political, social, and economic problems and gave sound advice to kings and officials in these fields. The better kings welcomed and sought such advice and counsel, whereas the wicked kings looked upon the prophets as enemies and obstacles in the way of carrying out their own nefarious purposes.

Many of the prophets in their visions and utterances rose above the immediate conditions of life about them and gave expression to basic truths that are of universal interest and application. A particularly prominent subject of prophecy was the coming of the Messiah and the glorious age which He would inaugurate. The Messianic idea dominated their view of the future.

In speaking of the prophets Dr. James Robertson says that while they were "men of their time," they were also "men above their time," and "men of all time."

Among the prophets a distinction is made between the *oral prophets,* who left no written records, and the *writing prophets,* whose words have been preserved in the Bible. Of the *oral prophets* mention may be made of such men as Nathan, Gad, Elijah, and Elisha who performed a large service.

In order to visualize the setting for the activities of the *writing prophets* it is helpful to associate them with the periods of history in which their work was done as follows:

PROPHETS IN ISRAEL
1. Jonah
2. Amos
3. Hosea

PROPHET IN ISRAEL AND JUDAH
1. Micah

PROPHETS IN JUDAH
1. Joel
2. Isaiah
3. Nahum
4. Zephaniah
5. Habakkuk
6. Jeremiah

116

Prophets During the Captivity

1. Ezekiel
2. Obadiah
3. Daniel

Prophets After the Captivity

1. Haggai
2. Zechariah
3. Malachi

Except in the case of the last three the order of the books in the Bible at the present time is not chronological. The order seems to have been determined mainly by the size of the books. The *major* books come first. The designations, *major* and *minor,* are not to be regarded, however, as an evaluation of the relative importance of the several prophets and their work.

The Biblical order of the Prophetical Books is as follows:

Major Books:

1. Isaiah
2. Jeremiah
3. Lamentations
4. Ezekiel
5. Daniel

Minor Books:

1. Hosea
2. Joel
3. Amos
4. Obadiah
5. Jonah
6. Micah
7. Nahum
8. Habakkuk
9. Zephaniah
10. Haggai
11. Zechariah
12. Malachi

CHAPTER XXXII

Isaiah: Trusting in God

THE MAN.—The name Isaiah means *Salvation is of Jehovah*. According to Jewish tradition Isaiah was of royal blood, being a grandson of Joash, king of Judah. He was prominent in public life for 60 years. As a prophet and statesman of commanding personality he wielded a tremendous influence for good during the reigns of four kings in Judah, Uzziah, Jotham, Ahaz and Hezekiah. According to tradition he died as a martyr during the reign of the succeeding king, Manasseh. Isaiah is generally regarded as the greatest of all the prophets.

THE SITUATION.—Isaiah lived during a very troubled period in the history of Israel. The Northern Kingdom, while outwardly rich and prosperous, was inwardly weak and corrupt. Unable to withstand attacks from without it broke under the pressure of the Assyrians, and Isaiah saw its people carried away into captivity by Salmanezer III.

Judah, too, was in grave danger from corruption within and enemies without. Isaiah labored valiantly to bring about reforms in religion and life. Against his positive advice to trust in the Lord and avoid "entangling alliances," King Ahaz entered into a protective alliance with Assyria. After destroying the Kingdom of Israel, however, Assyria proceeded to make a vassal of Judah. At a later time when the Assyrians threatened Jerusalem, King Hezekiah finally listened to Isaiah's advice to trust in God and the Assyrian army, under Sennacherib, was miraculously destroyed by an angel of Jehovah.

CONTENTS.—The 66 chapters in the book of Isaiah may be divided into two main divisions. The first 39 Chapters deal with historical events and conditions and the activities and prophecies of Isaiah under the four kings mentioned above. The second division, Chapters 40-66, contains prophecies regarding the deliverance from captivity in

Babylon and regarding the person, work, and glorious reign of the Messiah, the "Servant King."

Theme: Trusting in the Lord for Help and Salvation			
Isaiah's Activities and Prophecies			
Under Uzziah Chapters 1-5	Under Jotham Chapter 6	Under Ahaz Chapters 7-27	Under Hezekiah Chapters 28-39
Prophecies of Salvation			
Deliverance Chapters 40-48	The Ideal Servant King Chapters 49-53		The Ideal Kingdom Chapters 54-66

STUDY SUGGESTIONS

This survey must content itself with just a few notes on this magnificent book of vast and rich content.

I. ACTIVITIES OF ISAIAH UNDER UZZIAH. Chapters 1-5.

1. What information about the contents of the book is given in the title, v. 1:1?

2. Note the tremendous arraignment and call to repentance in 1:2-17.

3. What gracious invitation is extended in 1:18-20?

4. The rest of this section is occupied with further pictures of sin and punishment and the glories of a restored Judah. Note the beautiful prophecy, in 2:4, of the coming of the era of peace still to be attained.

II. ISAIAH'S VISION IN THE REIGN OF JOTHAM. Chapter 6.

1. What did Isaiah see and hear in this celebrated vision?

2. What thoughts does this vision suggest?

III. ACTIVITIES OF ISAIAH UNDER AHAZ. Chapters 7-27.

This section deals with the troubles besetting King Ahaz, the advice of Isaiah against "entangling alliances," and his prophecies of the fall of the world powers.

IV. ACTIVITIES OF ISAIAH UNDER HEZEKIAH. Chapters 28-39.

We have here prophecies of the fall of Assyria and Egypt and the fulfilment of the prophecy against Assyria. Read the brief but impressive account of the destruction of Sennacherib's army. 37: 36-38.

V. PROPHECIES OF DELIVERANCE. Chapters 40-48.

Isaiah here prophesies the restoration of Judah from the Babylonian captivity, but also goes far beyond that to a vision of the great deliverance under the Messiah.

VI. PROPHECIES CONCERNING THE IDEAL SERVANT KING. Chapters 49-53.

Messianic prophecy in this section visions salvation as coming not merely through Judah in a general way, but specifically through a particular individual, the ideal "Servant King," who unmistakably points to Christ. Read and meditate upon Chapter 53, the most remarkable prophecy of Christ in the Bible. It reads as if it were a picture of Christ's passion written after the event instead of hundreds of years beforehand.

VII. PROPHECIES OF THE IDEAL KINGDOM. Chapters 54-66.

In exalted prophecies sweeping over all time and space Isaiah here visions the glorious reign of the "Ideal King," the Messiah. It is truly remarkable that a Jew living when Isaiah did could see such things. The only possible explanation is that his mind was supernaturally illuminated by the Holy Spirit. It is not without reason that Isaiah has been called "The Evangelist of the Old Testament." Read and meditate upon the gracious invitation in Chapter 55.

NOTABLE PASSAGES IN ISAIAH

The Messianic idea is more prominent in Isaiah than in any other book in the Old Testament. Almost the whole career of Jesus is predicted. Some of the more definite passages are included in the following list.

Description of the People's Sins, Chapter 1. The Coming of the Messianic Kingdom, 2:1-5. Isaiah's Call, Chapter 6. The Virgin's Son, 7:14. The Prince of Peace, 9:1-7. The Branch Out of the Root of Jesse, Chapter 11. Christ's Forerunner, 40:1-8. The Greatness of God as compared with Idols, 40:9-31. The Humble Servant, Chapter 42. Christ's Redemption, Chapters 49-52. The Sufferings of Christ, Chapter 53. A Gracious Invitation, Chapter 55. The Messiah's Reign Pictured As the Year of Jubilee, Chapter 61 (Cf. Luke 4:14-21). The New Jerusalem, 65:17-25.

CHAPTER XXXIII

Jeremiah: The Fall of Jerusalem

THE MAN.—The name Jeremiah means *Exalted by Jehovah*. He was of a priestly family, designated even before birth to be a prophet of God. For fifty dark years in the history of Judah, before and after the fall of Jerusalem, he labored to bring his people to repentance, prophesied the doom in store for their sins and disobedience, but also spoke of the glory of the Messianic era. According to tradition he was stoned in Egypt by his own fellow exiles whom he had accompanied thither.

THE SITUATION.—When Jeremiah began his work the Northern kingdom, Israel, had been in captivity for 83 years. Judah too was fast degenerating through the deteriorating influence of infidelity, gross idolatry, and immorality. It was the hard and thankless task of Jeremiah to reprove the people for their sins and prophesy the certain doom that awaited them. This he continued to do during the reigns of Josiah, Jehoaz, Jehoiakim, Jehoiakin, and Zedekiah, until the capture of Jerusalem by Nebuchadnezzar. Jeremiah was therefore generally hated as a "prophet of doom," was persecuted, shamefully mistreated, and even imprisoned at times. But he remained true to his mission. He even comforted his unhappy countrymen by speaking of their return from Babylon and the ultimate salvation by the Messiah.

CONTENTS.—The book of Jeremiah opens with an account of the Prophet's divine call. The main body of the book is occupied with a setting forth of Judah's sins, calls to repentance, predictions of the Babylonian captivity and return, Messianic prophecies, the siege and fall of Jerusalem, and prophecies of the doom of many nations.

OUTLINE OF JEREMIAH

Theme: The Fall of Jerusalem			
The Prophet's Call Chapter 1	Events and Prophecies Before, During, and After the Fall of Jerusalem Chapters 2-45	Doom of Nations Chapters 46-51	Historical Conclusion Chapter 52

STUDY SUGGESTIONS

1. What facts about Jeremiah and the scope of this book do you find in 1:1-3?

2. Note in 1:4-5 that God had appointed Jeremiah to be a prophet even before he was born.

3. How was he equipped for his work? 1:6-9.

4. What was his work to be? 1:10.

5. What vision is reported in 1:11-12?

6. What vision in 1:13-16?

7. What hard experiences are predicted for Jeremiah in 1:17-19?

8. As a sample of the Lord's guidance of Jeremiah, the style of his teaching, and experiences with the impenitent people read Chapters 18 and 19.

9. Note the Messianic prophecy in 23:5-6.

10. As a sample of a wicked king's attitude to Jeremiah's prophesies read Chapter 36.

NOTABLE PASSAGES IN JEREMIAH

Jeremiah's Call, 1:1-10. The Vision of the Seething Pot. 1:13-19. Call to Repentance, Chapter 7. Prophecies of the Jews' Calamities, Chapter 8-9. The Potter's Vessel, Chapter 18. The Breaking of the Potter's Vessel, Chapter 19. "The Lord Our Righteousness," 23:5-8. The Return from Captivity, 29:10-14. The Restoration of Israel, Chapter 31.

CHAPTER XXXIV

Lamentations: Songs of Sorrow

AUTHOR.—Jeremiah.

OCCASION.—The Prophet was profoundly distressed over the fate that had befallen his beloved Jerusalem and his people in the victory of Nebuchadnezzar. Contemplating the ruin and desolation, he is moved to poetic expression of the sorrow that is in his heart, and with deep emotion he appeals to God for mercy and comfort.

CONTENTS.—The five chapters appear to be five songs which may be thought of as subdivisions of the main theme, as follows:

OUTLINE OF LAMENTATIONS

Theme: Sorrow Over the Fate of Jerusalem				
The Desolation of the City Chapter 1	The Reasons for Her Fall Chapter 2	Grounds of Consolation Chapter 3	Distress of the Siege Chapter 4	A Prayer for Mercy Chapter 5

STUDY SUGGESTIONS

In your reading note the deep emotion of the Prophet, his recognition of God's justice, and his hope of mercy for the penitent.

CHAPTER XXXV

Ezekiel: The Fall and Restoration of Jerusalem

THE MAN.—Ezekiel was a prophet and priest during the first period of the captivity in Babylon. He was a contemporary of Jeremiah and Daniel, his prophetic activities extending through 22 years. His name means *God strengthens me*. Learned, cultured, and deeply pious, he devoted himself conscientiously to the spiritual welfare of his people and came to hold a highly influential position among them.

THE SITUATION.—Ezekiel had been carried away into captivity to Babylonia, together with a large number of his countrymen, some years before the final destruction of Jerusalem. Many of these fellow captives believed that they would soon be permitted to return to Jerusalem; but it was the hard task of Ezekiel, by the Lord's direction, to prophesy the utter destruction of Jerusalem which actually took place in 587 B. C. He did, however, predict a return to Jerusalem, on the condition that the people would thoroughly repent of their idolatry and other sins. With great zeal he therefore preached repentance to them. The people turned away from the false gods and became fervently devoted to Jehovah and the true religion. Love for their sacred Scriptures was revived, and a general upturn in their religious life took place. In fact, idolatry, which had been so attractive to the Jews before, came ultimately to be regarded as the most hateful of all sins. Apparently they had been cured of it.

The conditions of the captivity were not hard. The Jews were allowed very considerable liberties as residents in Babylonia. They increased and prospered, and some of them rose to very high positions in the land. Religious freedom was allowed, and it is thought that the Synagogue worship developed during this period.

The devout Jews were unhappy, however, in their exile and longed with profound yearning for their beloved Jerusalem. Their attitude is given eloquent expression in Psalm 137, which should be read in this connection.

CONTENTS.—The book of Ezekiel consists mainly of groups of visions by which the Prophet was enabled to predict the hard fate of Jerusalem, the doom of nations that had oppressed Israel, and the return from captivity. The visions are rich in oriental imagery and some of them are very difficult to interpret. Aid to understanding is offered, however, by the suggestion that the visions cluster around the idea of the appearance, departure, and return of the *Glory of God,* an expression which occurs very frequently in the book.

OUTLINE OF EZEKIEL

Theme: The Fall and Restoration of Jerusalem			
The Prophet's Call and Commission Chapters 1-3	Predictions of the Fall of Jerusalem Chapters 4-24	Predictions of the Doom of the Nations Chapters 25-32	Predictions of the Restoration of Jerusalem Chapters 33-48

STUDY SUGGESTIONS

I. THE PROPHET'S CALL AND COMMISSION. Chapters 1-3.

1. What facts about the Prophet do you learn from 1:1-3?
2. A reading of these three chapters will give a vivid impression of the richness of imagery in Ezekiel's visions. It is a method of teaching which is difficult for the occidental mind to follow, but which delights the imagination of the oriental.

II. PREDICTIONS OF THE FALL OF JERUSALEM. Chapters 4-24.

The visions in this section set forth the impending destruction of Jerusalem together with the reasons for it.

III. PREDICTIONS OF THE DOOM OF THE NATIONS. Chapters 25-32.

The prophetic visions proclaim the judgments of God upon Ammon, Moab, Edom, Philistia, Tyre, Sidon, and Egypt because of their sins.

IV. PREDICTIONS OF THE RESTORATION OF JERUSALEM. Chapters 33-48.

In picturing the glory of the restored Jerusalem some of the visions in this section look forward to the still greater glory of the consummation of the kingdom of the Messiah.

NOTABLE PASSAGES IN EZEKIEL

The Prophet's Call, Chapters 1-3. The Righteousness of God's Dealings, Chapter 18. Rebuke of the False Shepherds, 34:1-19. The True Shepherd and Showers of Blessing, 34:20-31. Promises of God's Blessings, Chapter 36. The Valley of Dry Bones, 37:1-14.

CHAPTER XXXVI

Daniel: The Sovereignty of God

THE MAN.—Daniel, whose name means *God is my judge,* was carried away as a captive to Babylon when he was about sixteen years of age. He was from a Jewish family of high rank and a youth of fine promise, for he was chosen together with some other Jewish boys for special training at Nebuchadnezzar's court. Being a young man of deep piety, strong convictions, and courageous independence, he was able to withstand the temptations of an ungodly environment. Demonstrating remarkable qualities of intellectuality, wisdom, and leadership, he rose to the highest political position under the king and retained a place of very high authority in the Median and Persian empires, which in turn succeeded the Babylonian. As a prophet Daniel saw and interpreted remarkable visions. Although he did not himself return to Jerusalem, he had the joy of seeing the Babylonian captivity come to an end under Cyrus, king of Persia, and some 50,000 of his fellow countrymen return to their own beloved land. His political and prophetical activity extended over a period of 70 years.

THE SITUATION.—Being thrown into the main stream of world affairs, seeing one empire succeed another in dominance, Daniel was by God appointed to see and interpret the course of world history to the end of time, when the Messiah Kingdom was to be established forever. In the comprehensive sweep of his visions he looks not merely at the destiny of the Jew but at the whole course of humanity. The Messiah, the "Son of David," becomes here the "Son of Man."

THE CONTENTS.—The twelve chapters of Daniel fall naturally into two divisions. The first six chapters are of an historical nature recording events in the life of Daniel, told in the third person; the last six contain an account of four great visions, written in the first person. The central thought of the whole book is *the sovereignty of God.*

OUTLINE OF DANIEL

Theme: The Sovereignty of God	
Historical, Chapters 1-6. 1. Daniel's political training. Chapter 1. 2. Dream of the image and the stone. Chapter 2. 3. The golden image and the fiery furnace. Chapter 3. 4. Dream of the tree. Chapter 4. 5. Handwriting on the wall. Chapter 5. 6. In the Lion's den. Chapter 6.	Prophetical. Chapters 7-12. 1. Vision of the four beasts. Chapter 7. 2. Vision of the ram and the he-goat. Chapter 8. 3. Vision of the 70 weeks. Chapter 9. 4. Visions of nations and last things. Chapters 10-12.

STUDY SUGGESTIONS

A. HISTORICAL SECTION. Chapters 1-6.

I. DANIEL'S POLITICAL TRAINING—Chapter 1

1. What facts are stated in 1:1-2?
2. What instructions did Nebuchadnezzar give regarding certain Jewish young men? 1:3-7.

Daniel continues to be known chiefly by his old Jewish name, whereas the other three are best known by their new names: Shadrach, Meshach, and Abed-nego.

3. What light does the episode in 1:8-16 throw upon Daniel's character?
4. How do you account for the superiority of the four young men? 1:17-21.

II. THE DREAM OF THE IMAGE AND THE STONE
—Chapter 2

1. What demand did Nebuchadnezzar make of his wise men? 2:1-13.
2. What did Daniel do in this situation? 2:14-30.
3. What traits of Daniel are revealed in this section?
4. How did Daniel interpret the dream? 2:31-45.
5. To what position was Daniel promoted? 2:46-49.

Note on the Interpretation of Nebuchadnezzar's Dream.—The most generally accepted interpretation of Nebuchadnezzar's dream is as follows:

1. Head of gold—Babylonian Empire.
2. Breast and arms of silver—Medo-Persian Empire.
3. Belly and thighs of brass—Macedonian Empire.
4. Legs of iron and feet of iron and clay—The Roman Empire, with two divisions centering at Rome and Constantinople.
5. The stone—The Kingdom of Christ which shall be a universal and eternal kingdom.

III. THE GOLDEN IMAGE AND THE FIERY FURNACE
—Chapter 3

1. What decree did the king issue? 3:1-7.
2. What attitude did Shadrach, Meshach, and Abed-nego take? 3:8-23.
3. How were they delivered? 3:24-27.
4. Who was the fourth man seen with them in the furnace? 3:25.
5. What impression did the miracle make upon the king? 3:28-30.

IV. THE DREAM OF THE TREE—Chapter 4

1. What did Nebuchadnezzar see in his dream? 4:1-18.
2. How did Daniel interpret the vision? 4:19-27.
3. How was the dream fulfilled? 4:28-33.
4. What was the final effect upon the king? 4:34-37.

V. THE HANDWRITING ON THE WALL—Chapter 5

1. Of what profanation was Belshazzar guilty? 5:1-4.
2. What vision did he see? 5:5-9.
3. How did Daniel interpret this vision? 5:10-29.
4. What reasons did Daniel assign for Belshazzar's doom?
5. What was his fate? 5:30.

VI. IN THE LIONS' DEN—Chapter 6

1. What plot did the enemies of Daniel form? 6:1-9.
2. How did Daniel conduct himself in the difficult situation? 6:10-15.
3. How was he delivered? 6:16-24.
4. What decree did king Darius issue? 6:25-28.

B. The Prophetical Section. Chapters 7-12.

The limited scope of these Bible study helps does not allow of a consideration of the many problems associated

with the interpretations of Daniel's visions. The student
interested in pursuing a study of these visions should read
the accounts very carefully several times and get all he
can out of the reading. Then he may make judicious use
of able Bible commentaries. Students of Daniel's visions
should also study the book of *Revelation,* to which *Daniel*
serves as a prelude.

In a general way it may be stated that Daniel's visions
indicate a mighty conflict in the world between the forces
of evil and the forces of righteousness with the ultimate
complete victory of righteousness in the consummation of
the kingdom of Christ.

Note the reference to the *son of man* in 7:13-14 and to
the *Messiah,* or *the anointed one,* in 9:25.

NOTABLE PASSAGES IN DANIEL

Daniel's Training, Chapter 1. The Dream of the Image and the
Stone, Chapter 2. The Fiery Furnace, Chapter 3. The Dream of
the Tree, Chapter 4. The Handwriting on the Wall, Chapter 5.
Daniel in the Lions' Den, Chapter 6. The Vision of the Four
Beasts, Chapter 7. The "Son of Man," 7:13-14. The Messiah and
the Seventy Weeks, 9:20-27.

CHAPTER XXXVII

The Twelve Minor Prophets

For the purposes of comparison and reference there are set forth in the table below certain facts about the twelve books in the Bible known as the *Minor Prophets*.

THE TWELVE MINOR PROPHETS

Name	No. of Chapters	Location	Time	Theme
Hosea	14	In Israel	Shortly before fall of Israel	Unfaithfulness of Israel and call to repentance.
Joel	3	In Judah	About 100 years after Solomon	Repentance in anticipation of the Day of Judgment.
Amos	9	In Israel	Somewhat earlier than Hosea	Fall of Israel as a judgment for sin.
Obadiah	1	In Judah	At the time of the fall of Jerusalem	Judgment upon Edom for rejoicing over downfall of Jerusalem.
Jonah	4	In Israel	At height of its prosperity	God's mercy to repentant Nineveh.
Micah	7	In Israel and Judah	Shortly before fall of Israel	Punishment for injustice and idolatry.
Nahum	3	In Judah	After the fall of Israel	Prophecy of the destruction of Nineveh.
Habakkuk	3	In Judah	Shortly before fall of Judah	Vindication of God's righteousness in punishing sin.
Zephaniah	3	In Judah	Shortly before fall of Judah	The certainty of God's judgment upon sin.
Haggai	2	In Judah	After the return from captivity	To encourage completion of the Temple.
Zechariah	14	In Judah	After the return from captivity	Encouragement by prophecies of the glory of the Messianic kingdom.
Malachi	4	In Judah	After the return from captivity	To warn and encourage by picturing the righteousness and love of God

CHAPTER XXXVIII

Hosea: Unfaithfulness of Israel

THE MAN.—A man of deep emotions and righteous indignation, yet of tender sympathies for the penitent, Hosea labored among the people of the kingdom of Israel for a period of nearly 60 years.

THE SITUATION.—In a material and political way Israel was prosperous, but the spiritual and moral conditions were in a terrible state. Idolatry and all its accompanying vices prevailed among the people as never before. To bring about reforms in this deplorable situation it was that Hosea was commissioned, and he labored indefatigably through a long period of service. As the years went on, it became more and more clear that because the people would not repent and turn from their sins, the judgment of God would be visited upon them. It became, therefore, the task of Hosea as the servant of God to proclaim such judgment. It was his privilege, however, also to announce the restoration of an ultimately penitent Israel.

THE CONTENTS.—Under the figure of an adulterous wife Hosea pictures the religious unfaithfulness of Israel, calls them to penitence, and proclaims their doom. He also holds out a hope of better things if the people will repent.

OUTLINE OF HOSEA

Theme: The Unfaithfulness of Israel and Call to Repentance			
The Figure of the Adulterous Woman and the Call to Repentance Chapters 1-3	The Sins of Israel Rebuked Chapters 4-6	The Proclamation of Judgment Chapters 7-10	Blessings Received and Plea for Israel's Return to God Chapters 11-14

NOTABLE PASSAGES IN HOSEA

Judgments upon the Priests, 4:6-11. Exhortation to Repentance, Chapter 6. Destruction Threatened, Chapter 8. Israel's Ingratitude, Chapter 11. Promises to the Repentant, Chapter 14.

CHAPTER XXXIX

Joel: The Day of the Lord

THE MAN.—Little is known about the prophet Joel. He did his work in the kingdom of Judah, probably in Jerusalem. He was a contemporary of Elisha and probably knew Elijah also.

THE SITUATION.—The country was visited by a double calamity, a plague of locusts and a severe drought. Joel saw in these visitations the judgment of God on the sins of the people and made them an occasion for a powerful plea for repentance. Apparently the people did repent, and Joel was privileged to announce the grace of God and the return of prosperity to the country. Through his divinely illuminated insight the prophet saw in these events of his day also a type of what he called the *Day of the Lord,* when God on a world wide scale shall come to judgment, extending grace to the penitent and pronouncing doom upon the unrighteous. A part of this prophecy was fulfilled in the outpouring of the Holy Spirit on the day of Pentecost, whereas other portions of the prediction still await fulfillment.

THE CONTENTS.—The book sets forth the facts and interpretations referred to above. The descriptions of the plague and the drought and the desolations caused by them are regarded as unsurpassed in literature.

OUTLINE OF JOEL

Theme: The Day of the Lord			
The Calamities		The Day of the Lord	
The Plague and the Drought Chapter 1	Repentance and Grace 2:1-27	The Promise of the Spirit 2:28-32	Judgment, Punishment, and Blessing Chapter 3

133

STUDY SUGGESTIONS

1. Note the marvelous description of the plague of locusts and the drought in Chapter 1.

2. Note the prophecy of the outpouring of the Holy Spirit and the signs of the coming of the "Day of the Lord" in 2:28-32. According to the Apostle Peter this prophecy was at least in part fulfilled on the day of Pentecost. Cf. Acts 2:16-21.

NOTABLE PASSAGES IN JOEL

The Plague, 1:1-7. The Drought, 1:8-20. "The Day of the Lord," 2:1-11; Call to Repentance, 2:12-14. Prophecy of the Holy Spirit, 2:28-32. In the Valley of Decision, 3:14.

CHAPTER XL

Amos: Punishment

THE MAN.—Amos, when called to be a prophet, was a farmer living at Tekoa, a village not far from Jerusalem. He had no special school training for the office of prophet, but his natural talents of keenness and observation had been developed to a high degree in the school of the Spirit. These qualities, coupled with eloquence and courage and unquestioned obedience to the Lord's call, made him a power for righteousness among the people of his day. He was somewhat older than Hosea.

THE SITUATION.—While a native of Judah, Amos did his work in the kingdom of Israel during the reign of Jeroboam II. This king had been very successful in military conquest and had won back much of the territory that had been lost since the days of Solomon. The increased power, wealth, and sense of security in Israel had led to sins of every description. The basic sin was idolatry with its shameful practices. To rebuke the people for this and other sins and to proclaim punishment for their faithlessness was the commission which Amos received from the Lord. The prophet had an exalted and clear conception of the sovereignty of God over all the peoples and nations of the earth and boldly proclaimed judgment upon every nation that practiced idolatry and unrighteousness.

THE CONTENTS.—The book of Amos contains, in the first part, the prophet's proclamation of the Lord's punishment of the sins of the nations surrounding Israel and of Israel itself. In greater detail he sets forth the declaration of judgment upon Israel and visions of such judgment. Finally there is foretold the restoration of God's people. In Amos' bold denunciation of social and economic abuses among Israel he demonstrates the principle that true religion has definite social implications. Righteousness should make a difference in the relations of men, one to another.

OUTLINE OF AMOS

Theme: Punishment				
Punishment of Seven Nations 1:1—2:5	Punishment of Israel 2:6—2:16	Declaration of Judgment 3:1—6:14	Visions of Judgment 7:1—9:10	Restoration of God's People 9:11-15

NOTABLE PASSAGES IN AMOS

Judgment Upon Judah and Israel, 2:4-8. "Prepare to meet thy God," 4:12-13. Call to Repentance, 5:4-15. "Woe unto them that are at ease in Zion," 6:1-6.

CHAPTER XLI

Obadiah: Judgment Upon Edom

THE MAN.—We know practically nothing about Obadiah in addition to what this little book reveals. It seems clear that his prophecy was spoken after the fall of Jerusalem, and before the fall of Edom.

THE SITUATION.—The Edomites, who were the descendants of Esau, were continually hostile to the Israelites, the descendants of Jacob. When Jerusalem fell before Nebuchadnezzar, the Edomites not only rejoiced in the disaster of their brother people but actually joined the enemies of Israel in their career of plundering and murdering. For this shameful conduct Obadiah, as Jehovah's spokesman, pronounces the downfall of proud Edom. The prophecy was fulfilled through various military defeats, until the Edomite nation completely disappeared from the face of the earth—a striking illustration of the fate of those who deal badly with God's chosen people.

THE CONTENTS.—The book recites the crimes of Edom as over against Israel, proclaims its doom, and also foretells by contrast the glorious restoration of Judah.

OUTLINE OF OBADIAH

Theme: Judgment Upon Edom		
Proclamation of Judgment Vs. 1-9	Reasons for the Judgment Vs. 10-16	Restoration of Judah Vs. 17-21

NOTABLE PASSAGES IN OBADIAH

The Salvation of Judah, v. 17.

CHAPTER XLII

Jonah: God's Mercy to Repentant Nineveh

THE MAN.—Jonah was a prophet in the Northern kingdom, a member of the tribe of Zebulun, in the land of Galilee. He was active during the height of Israel's prosperity, in the reign of Jeroboam II.

THE SITUATION.—Nineveh, the capital of the Assyrian kingdom, was a notoriously wicked city, and Jonah was commissioned by Jehovah to go and proclaim its doom. Assyria was the arch-enemy of Israel, and Jonah wanted to see it destroyed. Fearing that the city might repent and be saved, Jonah tried to escape from the task which God had assigned to him.

THE CONTENTS.—The book records the Lord's commission to Jonah and the prophet's attempt to escape by a ship on which he took passage at Joppa. God, however, sent a very severe storm, and when it had been determined by lot that the storm was due to Jonah's presence aboard, the crew threw him into the sea. God sent a great fish which swallowed Jonah and after three days cast him upon the land. A second time Jehovah's orders came to Jonah, and this time he obeyed. When, as the result of his proclamation of doom, the people of Nineveh repented, Jonah became very angry with the Lord and was rebuked for the pettiness and the uncharitableness of his spirit.

The book constitutes an indictment of Hebrew exclusiveness, and makes strikingly clear the truth that Jehovah is God not only of Israel but of the Gentiles also, and is merciful to all truly repentant sinners.

The book of Jonah received specific historical verification by Jesus in that the prophet is made a type of Jesus Himself. (Cf. Matt. 12:38-41 and Luke 11:29-32.)

OUTLINE OF JONAH

Theme: God's Mercy to Repentant Nineveh			
Jonah's First Commission and Attempt to Escape Chapter 1	His Repentance Chapter 2	His Second Commission and the Repentance of Nineveh Chapter 3	Jonah's Anger and God's Rebuke Chapter 4

NOTABLE PASSAGES IN JONAH

Jonah's First Call and Disobedience, 1:1-3. Jonah's Second Call and Obedience, 3:1-4. Jonah's Anger and the Lord's Rebuke of Him, Chapter 4.

CHAPTER XLIII

Micah: Punishment for Injustice and Idolatry

THE MAN.—Micah was a younger contemporary of Isaiah. But whereas Isaiah belonged to the higher social strata, Micah was a man of the people. He worked both in Judah and Israel.

THE SITUATION.—Living in the times of Jotham, Ahaz, and Hezekiah, kings of Judah, Micah beheld with sorrow the idolatry, social injustice, and religious formalism prevailing both in Judah and Israel and employed all his earnest zeal and poetic eloquence to bring both rulers and people to repentance. This was shortly before the fall of Israel.

THE CONTENTS.—The prophet summons the people to appear before Jehovah as if for trial. He rebukes them in severest terms for their sins and calls upon them to repent. He sees also in prophetic vision the future glory of a restored Judah. Some of the most beautiful and significant Messianic prophecies in the entire Old Testament are found in this book.

The book seems to fall naturally into three divisions. The prophet addresses the capital cities, rulers, and people, respectively. Each division again sets forth judgment and holds out promises of mercy.

OUTLINE OF MICAH

Theme: Punishment for Injustice and Idolatry					
Trial of the Capital Cities Chapters 1-2		Trial of the Rulers Chapters 3:10—5:15		Trial of the People Chapters 6-7	
Judgment 1:2—2:11	Mercy 2:12-13	Judgment 3:1-12	Mercy 4:1—5:15	Judgment 6:1—7:13	Mercy 7:14-20

NOTABLE PASSAGES IN MICAH

The Promise of Peace, 4:1-4. Bethlehem the Birthplace of the Savior, 5:2. The Ideal of a Godly Life, 6:6-8. Trust in God, 7:5-7. The Grace of God, 7:18-19.

CHAPTER XLIV

Nahum: The Destruction of Nineveh

THE MAN.—Nahum was a native of Elkosh, in Galilee. Nothing further is known about this prophet than may be deduced from his prophecy, which was probably spoken in Jerusalem.

THE SITUATION.—Nineveh, the capital of Assyria, was at this time at the height of its power and glory, and also of its iniquity. For centuries the Assyrians as a great world power had harassed the people of Israel. Recently they had defeated and carried away the people of the Ten Tribes, and Jerusalem escaped destruction only by the Lord's intervention in the destruction of 185,000 of the Assyrian army besieging Jerusalem. The Assyrian kings were incredibly cruel. Myers quotes an inscription by their king Asshurbanipol as follows: "Their men, young and old, I took prisoners; of some I cut off the noses, ears and lips; of the young men's heads I made a tower; I exposed their heads as trophy in front of their city. The male children and the female children I burned in the flames."

The people of Nineveh repented temporarily on the occasion of the preaching of Jonah, but they fell back into idolatry and all forms of wickedness and openly defied God.

It was upon these people in the very midst of their power and dominion that Nahum boldly pronounced doom and destruction as punishment from Jehovah. And it was not long afterward that the dire prophecy was fulfilled, and Nineveh was laid in ruins so completely that 200 years later even her very name had been forgotten by the nations.

THE CONTENTS.—In its first part the book of Nahum sets forth the character of Jehovah as a kind of preamble to the prediction of doom. While Jehovah is good to those who take refuge in Him, He executes terrible judgment upon those who continually practice iniquity and defy Him. The book then predicts, in most vivid language, the impending doom and describes the piled up iniquities that made the punishment inevitable.

Outline of Nahum

Theme: The Destruction of Nineveh		
Character of Jehovah Chapter 1	The Punishment Chapter 2	Reasons for the Punishment Chapter 3

Notable Passages in Nahum

The Bringer of Good Tidings, 1:15.

CHAPTER XLV

Habakkuk: Vindication of God's Righteousness

THE MAN.—Habakkuk was a Levite as well as a prophet and carried on his ministry in Jerusalem, shortly before its downfall.

THE SITUATION.—Having attempted a reformation of his people, seemingly in vain, the prophet was troubled about the question as to why God permitted wickedness and violence to continue. His doubt was answered by the declaration that the Chaldeans would come and visit terrible judgment upon the people of Judah for their many sins. But this answer raised another question: Why should a more sinful people be used by God as a tool to punish a less sinful people? For the solution of this problem it was made plain to the Prophet that the cruel, corrupt, and haughty Chaldeans would in turn be punished in signal fashion for their sins. Thus are God's ways vindicated.

THE CONTENTS.—The book sets forth the two questions with their answers referred to above and closes with an exalted song of prayer for mercy, of praise in commemoration of God's wonderful dealings with His people, and of confidence in the salvation and strength of the Lord. In the midst of declarations of judgment on sin there is held out the joyous hope of God's believing children in the precious evangelical statement: "The righteous shall live by faith" (2:4). This passage, so central in the Christian system, was frequently quoted by Paul and Luther.

OUTLINE OF HABAKKUK

Theme: Vindication of God's Righteousness in Punishing Sin				
First Problem 1:2-11		Second Problem 1:12—2:20		Song of Prayer, Praise, and Confidence Chapter 3
The Prophet's Question 1:2-4	Jehovah's Answer 1:5-11	The Prophet's Question 1:12—2:1	Jehovah's Answer 2:2-20	

NOTABLE PASSAGES IN HABAKKUK

The Prophet's Problem, 1:2-4. Justification by Faith, 2:4. The Earth Shall Be Filled with the Knowledge of God, 2:14. The Futility of Idolatry, 2:18-20. The Prophet's Prayer, Chapter 3.

CHAPTER XLVI

Zephaniah: The Certainty of God's Judgment on Sin

THE MAN.—Zephaniah was a contemporary of Jeremiah, Nahum, and Habakkuk. He was deeply involved in the reformation which king Josiah attempted to bring about. He was of royal blood, a great grandson of Hezekiah. He is believed to have been a young man when this prophecy was spoken.

THE SITUATION.—While some of the people had responded sincerely to the urgent call to repentance, there was no general turning away from idolatry and immorality on the part of the great mass of the people. Josiah's reformation was of limited significance. It became the hard task of Zephaniah, therefore, to announce in unmistakable terms the certainty and scope of the coming punishment.

THE CONTENTS.—The book begins with the proclamation of doom upon Judah, then widens out to embrace judgment upon idolatrous and iniquitous peoples surrounding Judah on all sides. Along with the prophecies of punishment there goes, however, as in all the prophets, a wondrous promise of grace, deliverance, and restoration to the truly penitent.

OUTLINE OF ZEPHANIAH

Theme: The Certainty of God's Judgment Upon Sin			
Judgment Upon Judah		Judgment Upon the Nations	
The "Day of Wrath" and Its Causes 1:2-18	The Call to Repentance 2:1-3	The Doom of Moab, Philistia, Amon, Ethiopia, Assyria, Judah 2:4—3:7	Hope of Restoration for the Faithful Remnant 3:8-20

Notable Passages in Zephaniah

"The Day of the Lord," 1:14-18. Call to Repentance, 2:1-3. The Lord's Salvation, 3:14-20.

CHAPTER XLVII

Haggai: Encouragement to Rebuild the Temple

THE MAN.—Haggai was probably born in Babylon during the captivity and was among the remnant that returned to Jerusalem. He was a contemporary of Zechariah.

THE SITUATION.—At the time Haggai began his prophetic activity sixteen years had passed since the return of the exiles from captivity. At first the people had taken hold of the rebuilding of the Temple with vigor, but obstacles of various kinds came in the way, and the work ceased. The people continued, however, in a spirit of selfishness to build comfortable homes for themselves while the house of God lay in ruins. Calamities in the form of drought and crop failures came upon the land, and it was made clear to the people that these hard times were due to their disobedience and negligence.

It was to rebuke them for their religious sloth and to encourage them and their governor Zerubbabel to resume the work of rebuilding the Temple that Haggai was commissioned by God.

THE CONTENTS.—The book contains four messages which Haggai was inspired by God to proclaim, over a period of about four months. In these messages are set forth the facts and conditions indicated above.

OUTLINE OF HAGGAI

Theme: Encouragement to Rebuild the Temple			
First Message: Rebuke and Response Chapter 1	Second Message: The Glory of the Temple 2:1-9	Third Message: The Blessings of Obedience 2:10-19	Fourth Message: A Hopeful Promise 2:20-23

Notable Passages in Haggai

Rebuke of the People, 1:2-6. Encouragement, 2:4. Silver and Gold Are the Lord's, 2:8.

CHAPTER XLVIII

Zechariah: Encouragement by Prophecies of the Glory of the Messianic Kingdom

THE MAN.—Zechariah was a contemporary of Haggai and continued his work. He was of a priestly family and was born in Babylon

THE SITUATION.—The setting is the same as in the case of Haggai. But while Haggai as a practical man was concerned primarily with the material side of the rebuilding of the Temple, Zechariah deals more with the spiritual significance of the undertaking.

THE CONTENTS.—The book of Zechariah is highly symbolical, dealing much with visions and their meanings and prophecies of the future. Through these means the prophet, as the Lord's servant, would encourage the people in the midst of their present difficulties and distress by pointing to a splendid future in which enemies should be overthrown and the glory of a restored Judah should be realized. All this points unmistakably to the coming Messianic kingdom.

OUTLINE OF ZECHARIAH

Theme: Encouragement by Prophecies of the Glory of the Messianic Kingdom			
Introduction: Call to Repentance 1:1-6	Eight Visions Symbolic of the Future 1:7—6:15	The Right Observance and Meaning of Fast Days Chapters 7-8	The Future Glory of Judah Chapters 9-14

NOTABLE PASSAGES IN ZECHARIAH

The Golden Candlestick, Chapter 4. Good Works, 8:16-17. The King Entering Zion, 9:9 (Cf. Matt. 21:5). Messianic Prophecies, 13:1; 13:7. The Lord King Over All. 14:9.

CHAPTER XLIX

Malachi: Warning and Encouragement

THE MAN.—Nothing is known of Malachi except what may be inferred from this book. He is thought to have been a contemporary of Nehemiah, governor of Jerusalem. He is the latest of the Old Testament prophets.

THE SITUATION.—About a hundred years had passed since the time of Haggai and Zechariah. Both priests and people had become lax in their religious spirit. While they maintained the forms of religious observances, after a fashion, they were at heart worldly and indifferent and guilty of grave abuses as to sacrifices, tithes, and the requirements of the law. In some instances intermarriage with the heathen had taken place. Many had begun to have serious doubts about the fulfillment of the prophecies relating to a coming Savior.

THE CONTENTS.—By calling attention to the love and righteousness of God Malachi endeavors to call the people back from their spiritual delinquencies. Relative to the coming Deliverer Malachi speaks definitely of his forerunner, a prophecy which clearly points to John the Baptist. The prophet also pictures the day of the Messiah as a day of joy for the faithful but as a day of terror for the workers of iniquity.

Malachi stands, therefore, as a link between the Old and the New Testaments.

OUTLINE OF MALACHI

Theme: Warning and Encouragement		
The Love of God for Judah 1:1-5	Messages of Rebuke for Priests and People 1:6—2:17	Messages of Hope and Warning Chapters 3-4

Notable Passages in Malachi

The Greatness of the Lord's Name, 1:11. The Coming of the Messiah, 3:1-5. Stewardship, 3:8-11. The Lord's Jewels, 3:17. Judgment and Blessing, 4:1-3. The Second Elijah, 4:5-6.

CHAPTER L

Review

Having surveyed in brief the books of the Old Testament and noted something of their contents the student will do well at this point to review the ground covered so as to be able to think through the material in terms of the following items:

1. The names of the books in order and the general contents or theme of each book.

2. The course of the history of the people of Israel.

3. The development of the history of Redemption.

For reference there is listed below some of the significant dates in the history of Israel:

Call of Abraham..1921 B. C. (?)
The Exodus from Egypt.............probably 1320 B. C.
Establishment of the Monarchy......about 1050 B.C.
Disruption of the Monarchy........................ 931 B. C.
Fall of the Kingdom of Israel...................... 722 B. C.
Fall of the Kingdom of Judah................... 587 B. C.
End of the Captivity..................................... 517 B. C.

CHAPTER LI

The Inter-Testament Period

From the Babylonian Captivity to the Birth of Christ Palestine was a dependency under a series of empires, with the exception of a period of independence, for 103 years, under the leadership of the Maccabees.

The record is as follows:

1. Under Babylonia .... 70 years, 587-517 B. C.
2. Under Persia and Media .... 187 years, 517-330 B. C.
3. Under Macedonia .... 9 years, 330-321 B. C.
4. Under Egypt .... 123 years, 321-198 B. C.
5. Under Syria................................... 32 years, 198-166 B. C.
6. Under Maccabees .... 103 years, 166- 63 B. C.
7. Under Rome .... 59 years, 63- 4 B. C.

NOTES ON THE PERIODS

From the time of the Macedonian ascendency on, the Greek language and Greek culture were introduced into Palestine. Under Egypt, the first of the Ptolemies, Soter, transported 100,000 Jews to Alexandria, which city became an extremely important center of culture.

During the Egyptian rule, too, it was that the translation of the Old Testament into Greek, known as the Septuagint, was made. This was probably in the third century B. C.

During the Syrian supremacy there arose among the Jews the two sects, the Sadducees, favorable to Greek culture, and the opposing group, the Pharisees, who held tenaciously to Jewish traditions.

The extreme tyranny of the Syrian king, Antiochus Epiphanes, brought about the revolt and the independence of the Jews under the Maccabees.

Rome as the conqueror of the world added Palestine also to her dominions. Herod was placed as king over the country, and in order to gain favor with the Jews he began, in 19 B. C., to replace the old Temple with a new and more splendid one. In his reign was born Jesus Christ—the event around which all history centers.

CHAPTER LII

The New Testament

NAME.—When Jesus instituted the rite of Holy Communion He said: "This cup is the new covenant (testament) in my blood" (Luke 22:20). This was in contrast with the *old covenant* made with Moses (Exod. 24:8). From the above expression is derived the name *New Testament* to cover the second division of books in the Bible.

WRITERS.—9.

BOOKS.—27.

TIME WITHIN WHICH WRITTEN.—From about 50 to 100 A. D.

THEME.—The general themes of the New Testament books can best be shown by the use of the outline of the whole Bible previously employed, as follows:

THE BIBLE

Theme: Salvation Through Christ			
Old Testament	Gospels	Acts and Epistles	Revelation
Preparation of Salvation	Realization of Salvation	Application of Salvation	Culmination of Salvation

CONTENTS.—The New Testament books cover the life and work of Christ, the founding and early history of the Church, missionary activities, instructions in Christian doctrine and living, and the final consummation of the kingdom of Christ.

In relation to the Old Testament the New stands as fulfillment to promise, as superstructure to foundation, as

155

foliage and fruit to the roots of the plant. The revelations of God begun in the Old Testament are brought to completion in the New.

THE BOOKS AND THEIR GROUPINGS.—We may group the books of the New Testament as follows:

A. *Historical*—5 books.

1. Matthew
2. Mark
3. Luke
4. John
5. Acts

B. *Epistles*—21 books.

1. Romans
2. I Corinthians
3. II Corinthians
4. Galatians
5. Ephesians
6. Philippians
7. Colossians
8. I Thessalonians
9. II Thessalonians
10. I Timothy
11. II Timothy
12. Titus
13. Philemon
14. Hebrews
15. James
16. I Peter
17. II Peter
18. I John
19. II John
20. III John
21. Jude

C. *Prophetical*—1 book.

Revelation

CHAPTER LIII

The Four Gospels

Significant comparative facts about the four Gospels may be set forth in tabular form as below. For some parts of this table we are indebted to *The Travis Reference Harmony of the Four Gospels.*

THE FOUR GOSPELS

Name	About the Writer	Time of Writing	Place of Writing	Written to	To Show	Records Especially
Matthew	A Disciple, Formerly a Publican	60-70	Palestine	Jews	Jesus as the Messiah	Fulfilment of Prophecies
Mark	A Close Friend of Peter. Well-to-do	60-70	Rome (?)	Romans	Jesus as God because of His Power	Miracles
Luke	A Close Friend of Paul. A Physician	60-70	Caesarea (?)	Greeks	Jesus as Savior of All	Parables
John	A Disciple. Formerly a Fisherman	85-100	Ephesus (?)	Early Christians	Jesus as the Son of God	Discourses of Jesus

THE FOUR GOSPELS (Continued)

Name	Genealogy of Jesus Traced to	Characterized by	Point of View as to Time	No. of Chapters
Matthew	Abraham	Reverence for the Old Testament	The Past	28
Mark	No Genealogy	Rapidity of Movement	The Present	16
Luke	Adam	Universality	The Future	24
John	God	Spirituality	Eternity	21

The first three Gospels are called the *Synoptic (seeing together) Gospels* because they give largely similar accounts of Jesus' life and work. The fourth Gospel, written considerably later, differs from the first three by omitting much that they contain and by including much that they leave out.

The four Gospels may be outlined as follows:

THE GOSPEL OF MATTHEW

Theme: Jesus the Messianic King			
The Introduction of the King 1:1—4:11	The Teachings and Works of the King 4:12—16:20	The Passion and Death of the King 16:21—27:66	The Resurrection of the King 28

THE GOSPEL OF MARK

Theme: Jesus the Mighty Son of God			
Introduction: The Beloved Son 1:1-13	His Great Works 1:14—10:52	His Passion and Death 11-15	His Resurrection 16

THE GOSPEL OF LUKE

Theme: Jesus the Savior of All			
His Birth and Early Life 1-2	His Ministry and Teachings for Jews and Gentiles 3-19	His Passion and Death 20-23	His Resurrection 24

THE GOSPEL OF JOHN

Theme: Jesus the Eternal Son of God				
His Pre-existence 1:1-18	His Public Ministry 1:19—12:50	His Private Ministry 13-17	His Passion and Death 18-19	His Resurrection and Appearances 20-21

158

CHAPTER LIV

The Life of Christ

On the basis of the four Gospels we shall endeavor to get before us in a fairly comprehensive way the main events in the life of Christ and consider something of the meaning of these events. We shall also take note of some of Jesus' teachings.

We shall use materials from all four of the Gospels, piecing them together so as to get a harmonious whole view of the earthly career of Jesus.

As an aid to the memory and as a framework into which to fit the materials of study there is submitted below a concise outline of the life of Christ.

For some features of our study we gratefully acknowledge our indebtedness to the *Oxford Cyclopedic Concordance*.

BRIEF OUTLINE OF THE LIFE OF CHRIST

I. The Pre-existence of Jesus Christ as the Eternal Word.

II. The Genealogy of Jesus.

III. The Annunciation to Zacharias of the Birth of John, the Forerunner of Jesus.

IV. The Annunciation to Mary of the Birth of Jesus.

V. The Birth of John.

VI. The Birth and Childhood of Jesus.

VII. Preparations for His Ministry.

VIII. The First Year of His Ministry. Age 31. A Year of beginnings and obscurity. Spent largely in Judea.

IX. The Second Year of His Ministry. Age 32. A year of setting forth fundamental principles. A period of popularity. Spent largely in Galilee.

X. The Third Year of His Ministry. Age 33. A year of change from popularity to hostility. Mighty deeds amid great opposition. Spent largely in Galilee and Peraea.

XI. The Last Three Months. Spent largely in retirement in Peraea.

XII. The Last Week. Culmination of opposition in the Crucifixion.

XIII. The Resurrection and Appearances.

XIV. The Ascension.

STUDY SUGGESTIONS

With the above brief outline as a guide let us proceed to consider in some detail the materials of the Gospels. In the case of parallel accounts we have selected as a rule the record in only one Gospel, usually the most complete one.

I. THE PRE-EXISTENCE OF JESUS CHRIST AS THE ETERNAL WORD (John 1:1-18).

1. What three great facts about the Word are stated in v. 1?
2. What additional facts are stated in 2-13?
3. What is the meaning of v. 14?

II. THE GENEALOGY OF JESUS (Matt. 1:1-17; Luke 3:23-38).

1. Note that Matthew traces the genealogy of Jesus back to Abraham, while Luke traces it back to Adam. Why this difference?
2. There are also differences in the genealogies in the period between David and Jesus. Apparently Matthew gives the genealogy of Joseph, the legal father of Jesus, while Luke gives the genealogy of Mary, the actual mother of Jesus. Both Joseph and Mary were of Davidic descent, Joseph through David's son, Solomon; and Mary through David's son, Nathan.

III. THE ANNUNCIATION TO ZACHARIAS OF THE BIRTH OF JOHN, THE FORERUNNER OF JESUS (Luke 1:5-25).

1. Who was Zacharias? 5.
2. What was his wife's name?
3. What information about them is given in vs. 6-7?
4. What message did the angel Gabriel deliver to Zacharias? 8-17.

5. How did he receive the message? 18.

6. What punishment came to him because of his lack of faith? 19-23.

IV. THE ANNUNCIATION TO MARY OF THE BIRTH OF JESUS (Luke 1:26-56).

1. What is the gist of the angel's message to Mary? 1:26-38.

2. What is stated about Jesus? 32-33.

3. During the visit of Mary to Elizabeth (39-45) what knowledge does Elizabeth reveal?

4. The Song of Mary (46-55) is the "Magnificat," so named from its first word in the Latin version. What are its main ideas?

5. What impression of Mary do you get?

V. THE BIRTH OF JOHN (Luke 1:57-80).

1. How did the naming of John impress the relatives and neighbors? 57-66.

2. Note the beautiful song composed by Zacharias. 67-79. What is its central thought?

3. What facts are stated about John in v. 80?

VI. THE BIRTH AND CHILDHOOD OF JESUS (Luke 2:1-52; Matt. 2:1-23).

1. By what historical event was the time of Jesus' birth fixed? Luke 2:1-7.

Note on the date of the birth of Jesus. The date of Jesus' birth is usually placed at 4 B. C. This is perplexing unless we know the facts in the case. The explanation is as follows. Dates were not counted from the birth of Christ until many centuries after that event. In that part of the world time was usually counted from the founding of Rome. In 526 A. D. a monk by name Dionysius Exiguus published calculations to the effect that Jesus was born 754 years after the founding of Rome. That date was therefore made the year 1 of the Christian era, and from that time on dates throughout Christendom were counted before or after that year. Later, however, it was discovered that the monk had made an error in his calculations and that Jesus was born four years earlier than he had figured out. This made an adjustment necessary, but instead of changing all the dates in history, the practice has been followed of moving the date of the birth of Jesus back from the year 1 to the year 4 B. C.

2. How did it come about that Jesus was born in Bethlehem? Luke 2:1-5.

3. What thoughts are suggested by the lowly circumstances of Jesus' birth? Luke 2:6-7.

4. Why do you suppose the angel's announcement of the birth of Jesus was made to the shepherds rather than to other people? Luke 2:8-14.

161

5. What was the content of the announcement?

6. The beautiful song of the angels is called the *Gloria* from the first word in the Latin version of it.

7. What traits of the shepherds are revealed by their visit to Bethlehem? Luke 2:15-20.

8. What do you note in Luke 2:19?

9. Note that Jesus was circumcised at the age of eight days. Luke 2:21. Circumcision was the rite then in vogue for bringing people into covenant relations with God. Later on baptism replaced circumcision.

10. The name *Jesus* means *Savior*.

11. By whom was Jesus recognized in the Temple when He was presented there at the age of forty days? Luke 2:22-38. How were they affected?

12. The prayer song of Simeon is called the *Nunc Dimmittis* from the first two words of the Latin version.

13. How were the wise men guided to find Jesus? Matt. 2:1-12.

14. What is stated about them in Matt. 2:11?

15. The wise men may be regarded as representatives of the gentile world. The festival *Epiphany*, meaning *appearance*, is observed in the Christian church, on January 6th, in commemoration of the visit of the wise men; and the cause of foreign missions is appropriately stressed on that day.

16. What was the reason for the flight of Joseph's family to Egypt? Matt. 2:13-15.

17. What terrible act by King Herod is recorded in Matt. 2:16-18?

18. Returning from Egypt where did Joseph's family go to live? Matt. 2:19-23. Nazareth, as the home of Jesus during His childhood and youth, has connected with it most hallowed associations in the minds of Christians everywhere.

19. What significant episode is recorded in Luke 2:41-51?

20. In what four ways did Jesus develop according to Luke 2:52? We have here a comprehensive educational program.

VII. Preparations for Jesus' Ministry. Age 30.

1. Who prepared the way for Jesus? Matt. 3:1-12. The Ministry of John the Baptist began half a year before Jesus' ministry and continued parallel with it for about one year and three months.

2. What was unusual about the personal habits of John? Matt. 3:4.

3. What was the main theme of his preaching?

4. Where and by whom was Jesus baptized? Matt. 3:13-17.

5. How was the Trinity represented at the baptism of Jesus?

6. What types of temptation are represented by the tests to which Jesus was subjected? Matt. 4:1-11.

7. How did Jesus drive back the tempter?

VIII. The First Year of Jesus' Ministry. Age 31, A Year of Beginnings and Obscurity. Spent Largely in Judea.

1. The Testimony of John the Baptist. John 1 :19-34.

a) What did John assert and deny in relation to himself and Jesus? John 1 :19-28.

b) What testimony about Jesus did he offer? John 1 :29-34.

2. The first disciples. John 1 :35-51.

a) Who became Jesus' first followers?

b) State how each one was led to Jesus. What suggestions for personal work do these experiences contain?

3. The first miracle. John 2 :1-12.

a) What was the first miracle performed by Jesus?

b) What do you make of Jesus' words to His mother in v. 4?

c) What thought is suggested by the words of the ruler of the feast in 9-10?

4. The first cleansing of the Temple. John 2 :13-25.

a) What bold act of Jesus is recorded in John 2 :13-17? What impression of Jesus does this episode give? John 2 :18-25.

b) What sign of His authority did Jesus give? John 2 :18-25.

5. The first recorded discourse. John 3 :1-21.

a) John 3 :1-21 records the first discourse of Jesus of considerable length. Why do you suppose Nicodemus came to Jesus by night?

b) What was the gist of the conversation?

c) What event in the Old Testament is referred to in 14-15? Cf. Numbers 21 :4-9.

d) Why is John 3 :16 a precious verse?

6. Activities of John the Baptist. John 3 :22-36.

a) What light is thrown upon the character of John the Baptist in John 3 :22-36?

7. Jesus in Samaria. John 4 :1-38.

a) What light is thrown upon Jesus as a soul-winner by His dealings with the Samaritan woman? John 4 :1-26.

b) What resulted from the conversion of the Samaritan woman? John 4 :27-42.

c) What glimpse into the Savior heart of Jesus does the passage John 4 :31-38 give?

8. The healing of the nobleman's son. John 4 :43-54.

a) What was unique about this miracle?

IX. The Second Year of Jesus' Ministry. Age 32. A Year of Setting Forth Fundamental Principles. A Period of Popularity. Spent Largely in Galilee.

1. Jesus' visit to His home town. Luke 4:14-30.

a) What life habit did Jesus observe in Nazareth? Luke 4:16.

b) What light is thrown upon His attitude to the Old Testament? Luke 4:17-21.

c) Why did His fellow-townsmen turn against Him? Luke 4:22-30.

2. Jesus in Capernaum. Luke 4:31-44.

a) Being rejected in Nazareth, Jesus took up His abode in Capernaum, and this city became, in a sense, His headquarters. Where was it located?

b) What impression did His teaching produce? Luke 4:31-32.

c) What miracles did He perform at this time? Luke 4:33-41.

d) What need did Jesus feel? Luke 4:42-44.

3. Jesus' Ministry in Galilee. Luke 5:1—6:19.

a) In what connection did Jesus call disciples to become "Fishers of men"? Luke 5:1-11.

b) Of what is leprosy a symbol? Luke 5:12-13.

c) Why did Jesus tell the healed leper not to spread the report of His healing? Luke 5:14-16.

d) What claims did Jesus make for Himself in connection with the healing of the paralytic? Luke 5:17-26.

e) From what kind of an occupation was Levi (Matthew) called? Luke 5:27-28.

f) What is the meaning of Jesus' words in Luke 5:31-32?

g) How do you interpret the parables in Luke 5:33-39?

h) What view of the Sabbath did Jesus take? Luke 6:1-11.

4. The calling of the twelve disciples. Luke 6:12-19.

a) What did Jesus do before calling His disciples? Luke 6:12-13.

b) Name the twelve disciples. Luke 6:14-19.

5. The sermon on the Mount. Matt. 5-7.

a) Memorize the nine Beatitudes. Matt. 5:1-12.

b) How may Christians be "salt" and "light"? Matt. 5:13-16.

c) What does Jesus add to the old moral standards? Matt. 5:17-48.

d) What warning does Jesus give in connection with alms, prayer, and fasting? Matt. 6:1-18.

e) Note the giving of the Lord's Prayer. Matt. 6:9-15.

f) What verse summarizes the content of Matt. 6:19-34?

g) What common fault does Jesus criticize in Matt. 7:1-5?

h) How do you understand Matt. 7:6?

i) What remarkable promises are found in Matt. 7:7-12? Cf. Matt. 7:11 with Luke 11:31. What new idea is presented in Luke?

j) To what does the "narrow gate" and "strait way" lead? Matt. 7:13-14.

k) What is the essence of the warning in Matt. 7:15-23?

l) What lesson is taught by the parable of the two builders? Matt. 7:24-27.

m) What impression did Jesus' teaching produce? Matt. 7:28-29.

6. Jesus' Continued Ministry in Galilee. Luke 7-8.

a) What was remarkable about the Centurion's faith? Luke 7:1-10.

b) What spiritual experience is suggested by the episode in Luke 7:11-17? Cf. Ephesians 2:1-6.

c) What was John the Baptist's difficulty? Luke 7:18-35.

d) What was Jesus' estimate of him?

e) What do you note in comparing Simon the Pharisee with the sinful woman? Luke 7:36-50.

f) What facts are stated in Luke 8:1-3?

g) The section, Luke 8:4-16, contains some parables. A fuller account of these is found in Matt. 13, which chapter is remarkable for its record of eight parables of the Kingdom.

h) What impression on the disciples did Jesus' stilling of the storm produce? Luke 8:22-26.

i) What three miracles of Jesus are recorded in Luke 8:26-56? Note that they were performed on a man, a woman, and a child, suggesting the truth that Jesus is the Savior of all.

X. The Third Year of Jesus' Ministry. Age 33. A Year of Change from Popularity to Hostility, Mighty Deeds amid Great Opposition. Spent Largely in Galilee and Peraea.

1. Activities in Galilee. Mark 6:1—7:23.

a) What attitude on the part of the people did Jesus find on His second return to His home town? Mark 6:1-6.

b) Why did Jesus send out His disciples by two and two? Mark 6:7-13.

c) What instructions did He give them?

d) State the circumstances of the death of John the Baptist. Mark 6:14-29.

e) What miracle is recorded in Mark 6:30-44?

Note on the popular conception of the Messiahship.—The effect produced by the miracle of the feeding of the 5,000 marks the highest point in the popularity of Jesus. The miracle is recorded by all four Evangelists. In John 6:15 we are told that Jesus, perceiving that the people were about to come and take Him by force, to make Him king, withdrew again into the mountain Himself alone. Through mistaken guidance by their leaders the people had come to hold the idea that the Messiah was to be an earthly monarch who would set up the mightiest kingdom in the history of the world, a kingdom that should endure forever. In the presence of this erroneous conception, Jesus faced the problem of setting forth the essentially spiritual nature of His kingdom, a conception which it was difficult even for the disciples to grasp clearly. In fact, their understanding of the idea was apparently not clarified until the illumination of the Holy Spirit came to them on the day of Pentecost. Jesus' withdrawal from the crowd in the midst of the wave of popular favor, following the miracle of the feeding of the 5,000, was to avoid their crowning Him as a temporal monarch. His discouraging of the people along this line and His subsequent efforts to show them the spiritual nature of His kingdom caused many to turn away. The wave of popularity passed over very soon into open hostility.

f) Why did Jesus let the disciples struggle on the sea so long before coming to them? Mark 6:45-52.

g) How did the sick people show their faith in Jesus? Mark 6:53-56.

h) What is the main idea in the discourse about washing before eating? Mark 7:1-23.

2. Jesus' Retirement into Phenicia and Return to Galilee. Mark 7:57—8:26.

a) What evidence of faith did the Syro-Phenician woman show? Mark 7:24-30.

b) Why did Jesus use the method He did in healing the deaf-mute? Mark 7:31-37.

c) What differences are there in the accounts of the feeding of the 4,000 and the 5,000? Mark 8:1-10. Cf. Mark 6:30-46. Cf. also Mark 8:14-21.

d) What is meant by Mark 8:15? Cf. Matt. 22:15-22.

e) What spiritual experiences are suggested by the steps in the healing of the blind man? Mark 8:22-26.

3. Peter's Great Confession at Caesarea Philippi. Matt. 16:13-28.

a) What was the content of Peter's great confession? Matt. 16:13-20.

b) What progress in understanding of Jesus does Peter's confession indicate?

c) How did Jesus receive the confession?

d) What prediction does Jesus make regarding the future? For Himself and the disciples? Matt. 16:21-28.

e) What was Peter's reaction?

4. The Transfiguration of Jesus. Luke 9:28-43.

a) Why, do you suppose, were the disciples permitted to see the transfiguration of Jesus? Luke 9:28-36.

b) What do you think of Peter's proposal?

c) Compare the scene on the mount of transfiguration with the scene following in the valley below. Luke 9:37-43.

d) What lessons from those situations may be applied to our own lives?

e) What do you note in Luke 9:51.

5. Jesus in Jerusalem. John 7:1—10:21.

a) What does John 7:1-13 tell about Jesus?

b) What attitude toward Jesus is developing in 7:14—8:59?

c) What claims does Jesus make for Himself in this section?

d) What problem did the healing of the blind man raise for the enemies of Jesus? John 9.

e) Compare John 10:1-21 with Psalm 23.

6. The Mission of the Seventy. Luke 10:1-24.

a) What instruction did Jesus give the seventy emissaries? 10:1-16.

b) What success did they have? Luke 10:17-20.

c) How do you understand Jesus' words in Luke 10:21-24?

7. Jesus' visit in the Bethany home? Luke 10:38-42.

a) What difference do you note between Martha and Mary?

b) What did Jesus mean by the statement: "One thing is needful"?

XI. The Last Three Months of Jesus' Ministry. Spent Largely in Retirement in Peraea.

1. Jesus retires beyond the Jordan. John 10:40-42.

a) What facts are stated about Jesus in John 10:40-42?

b) During His sojourn in Peraea Jesus set forth many beautiful parables that are recorded in Luke 14-16.

2. The raising of Lazarus. John 11.

a) Why did Jesus delay after hearing about the illness of Lazarus? John 11:1-7.

b) What do verses 21 and 32 reveal?

c) Note v. 35, the shortest verse in the Bible.

d) What is the best verse in this chapter?

e) Jesus raised three people from the dead, the widow's son at Nain, the daughter of Jairus, and Lazarus. From the human point of view how do they compare in difficulty?

f) What effect did the raising of Lazarus have upon the enemies of Jesus? John 11:46-53.

g) What did Jesus do? John 11:54-57.

3. Events in connection with Jesus' last journey to Jerusalem.

a) What is stated about Jesus and His disciples in Luke 17:1-10?

b) How did the one leper differ from the other nine? Luke 17-11-19.

c) What time or event is referred to in Luke 17:20-37?

d) Why did Jesus tell the story of the unjust judge? Luke 18:1-8.

e) What points of difference do you find between the Pharisee and the Publican? Luke 18:9-14.

f) What light does Luke 18:15-17 throw upon Jesus? Cf. Mark 10:13-16.

g) What attitude toward money does Jesus set forth in connection with the encounter with the rich young ruler? Luke 18:18-30.

h) What prediction does Jesus make in Luke 18:31-34?

i) Why did Jesus ask the question of the blind man? Luke 18:35-43.

j) What evidences of sincerity does Zacchaeus show? Luke 19:1-10.

k) What lesson does the parable of the pounds teach? Luke 19:11-27.

XII. Events of the Last Week of Jesus' Earthly Life. Culmination of Opposition in the Crucifixion.

1. Jesus' triumphal entry into Jerusalem.

a) What was especially significant about Jesus' entry into Jerusalem? Matt. 21:1-11.

b) If Jesus had wanted to, He could easily have been made king at this time. Instead of complying with the wishes of the people what did He do? Why? Matt. 21:12-17.

2. Jesus' public teaching during the last week. Matt. 21:23— 25:46.

During these last days Jesus set forth some of His best known teachings. Among them the following parables: Two Sons, the Wicked Husbandmen, The King's Marriage Feast, The Ten Virgins, The Talents. In addition to setting forth the parables He engaged in discussions with the Pharisees and Sadducees and exposed their sins before the people. Note the seven-fold woes, in Matt. 23, pronounced against the Scribes and Pharisees. Jesus also foretold events connected with His second coming and the last judgment. The opposition of His enemies continued to develop in intensity and issued in definite plans for putting Him to death. Note Jesus' grief over Jerusalem, expressed in Matt. 23:37-39.

3. The Greeks seek Jesus. John 12:20-36.

a) What is the significance of the request of the Greeks?

b) How did the request affect Jesus?

c) How do you interpret John 12:32?

4. The anointing of Jesus in Bethany. Matt. 26:6-13.

a) How did Jesus interpret His anointing?

b) What prophecy in this connection has been fulfilled?

5. The bargain of Judas Iscariot. Matt. 26:14-16.

a) With whom did Judas make his bargain?

b) How much money was he to receive?

6. The institution of the Lord's Supper.

a) What preparations were made for the Paschal Supper? Luke 22:7-13.

b) What lesson did Jesus teach by His foot washing? John 13:1-17.

c) What statements did Jesus make in connection with the offering of the bread and wine? Luke 22:14-20. Cf. 1 Cor. 11:23-29

d) How did Jesus reveal the fact that He knew of Judas' plot to betray Him? John 13:21-30.

e) What profession of loyalty did Peter make? John 13:31-38.

f) What prediction regarding him did Jesus make?

7. The farewell discourses of Jesus with His disciples. John 14-16.

a) Make a list of the promises in John 14.

b) What great spiritual truth is taught in John 15:1-17?

c) What prospect is held before the disciples in John 15:18-27?

d) What did Jesus say would be the work of the Holy Spirit? John 16:1-15.

e) How do you explain John 16:7?

f) What was Jesus' purpose in telling about His going away? John 16:16-33. Note especially v. 33.

8. Jesus' High Priestly Prayer. John 17.

a) This prayer may be divided into three parts: 1-5; 6-19; and 20-26. State for whom and what Jesus prays in each of these divisions.

b) Note especially significant passages in this prayer.

9. Jesus' agony in Gethsemane. Matt. 26:36-46.

a) What are the evidences of Jesus' agony? Cf. Luke 22:44.

b) Why did Jesus pray as He did?

10. The betrayal and arrest of Jesus. Matt. 26:47-56.

a) How was Jesus betrayed?

b) Why did He oppose the use of force in defending Him?

11. The Jewish trial. Matt. 26:57-75.

a) On what grounds was Jesus condemned to die? Matt. 26:57-66.

b) How was He treated? Matt. 26:67-68.

c) How was Jesus' prediction regarding Peter fulfilled? Matt. 26:69-75. What was the cause of Peter's downfall? What do you note in v. 75?

12. The Roman trial.

a) Before whom was Jesus brought for the second trial? Matt. 27:1-2.

b) What was the reason for the double trial?

c) What was Judas' fate? Matt. 27:3-10. Was he truly repentant?

d) What was Pilate's judgment concerning Jesus? Luke 23:1-5.

e) Why was Jesus sent to Herod? Luke 23:6-12.

f) Why did Jesus refuse to answer Herod's questions?

g) When Jesus was returned, how did Pilate try to release Him? Matt. 27:14-26.

h) What message did Pilate receive from his wife? Matt. 27:19.

i) What was Pilate's final decision? Matt. 27:26.

j) To what insults was Jesus subjected? Matt. 27:27-32.

13. On the way to Calvary.

a) Who was compelled to carry Jesus' Cross? Luke 23:26.

b) What did Jesus mean by His words to the people who followed Him? Luke 23:27-31.

c) What fact is stated in Luke 23:32?

14. The Crucifixion.

a) The Hebrew name for the hill where Jesus was crucified is *Golgatha,* whereas from the Latin name is derived our word, *Calvary.* Luke 23:33.

b) What was the superscription on the cross? John 19:19-22.

c) What was Jesus' *first word* from the cross? Luke 23:34.

d) What did the soldiers do with Jesus' clothes? John 19:23-24.

e) How was Jesus mocked while on the cross? Matt. 27:39-44.

f) What was Jesus' *second word* from the cross? Luke 23:39-43.

g) What was the *third word* from the cross? John 19:25-27.

h) What phenomenon of nature occurred at this time? Matt. 27:45.

i) What was the *fourth word* from the cross? Matt. 27:46-47.

j) What was the *fifth word?* John 19:28-29.

k) What was the *sixth word?* John 19:30a.

l) What was the *seventh word?* Luke 23:46.

m) What phenomena accompanied Jesus' death? Matt. 27:50-53.

n) What impression did Jesus' death make on the onlookers? Matt. 27:54.

o) What precaution did the soldiers take to make sure that Jesus was actually dead? John 19:31-37.

15. The burial and the watch.

a) Where and by whom was Jesus buried? John 19:38-42. Cf. Matt. 27:57-61.

b) What action did the enemies of Jesus take in regard to the sepulchre? Matt. 27:62-66.

XIII. THE RESURRECTION AND APPEARANCES OF JESUS.

1. The Resurrection.

a) The resurrection of Jesus is recorded by all the Evangelists as follows: Matt. 28:1-10; Mark 16:1-8; Luke 24:1-12; John 20:

1-18. It is somewhat difficult to fix the order of events in these records of Easter morning, but one fact is abundantly clear—that Jesus arose from the dead.

b) Read the account in Matt. 28:1-10 and note the facts stated there.

c) What was done when the guards brought reports of the resurrection to the chief priests? Matt. 28:11-15.

2. The appearances of Jesus.

a) According to the records Jesus appeared in the morning of Easter day to Peter and several of the women.

b) In the evening He appeared to two disciples at Emmaus. Read this account in Luke 24:13-35 and note the circumstances and facts recorded.

c) What is significant to note in connection with Jesus' appearance as recorded in Luke 24:36-49?

d) How did Jesus deal with Thomas' doubt as to the resurrection? John 20:24-29.

e) What interesting circumstances are connected with the appearance recorded in John 21:1-23?

f) What commission is recorded in Matt. 28:16-20?

XIV. THE ASCENSION OF JESUS.

a) From what place did Jesus' ascension take place? Luke 24:50-53.

b) What was the manner of His ascension?

c) What statement about Jesus' return is found in the account of the ascension in Acts 1:6-11?

ADDITIONAL STUDY SUGGESTIONS

If time is not available for a study of the Life of Christ as outlined in the previous pages, certain materials in the Gospels may be selected for briefer study. Among the many possibilities may be mentioned the following:

1. Chief events in the life of Christ, such as His birth, visit in the Temple at twelve, His baptism, temptation, first preaching, first miracles, Sermon on the Mount, Peter's Great Confession, the transfiguration, triumphal entry into Jerusalem, farewell discourses, agony in Gethsemane, arrest, trials, crucifixion, death, burial, resurrection, ascension. References for these features of Jesus' life may readily be found in the foregoing outline.

2. A study of Christ's teachings on various subjects, by the aid of a *Concordance* or *Topical Textbook.*

3. A study of the miracles of Jesus.

4. A study of the parables of Jesus.

5. A study of notable passages in the Gospels.

6. Location of chief places visited by Jesus. See map, page 176.

For the sake of convenient reference there are listed here the *miracles* performed by Jesus that are recorded in the Gospels and the *parables* spoken by Him together with a brief statement of the leading lesson taught by each parable. We are indebted to the *Oxford Cyclopedic Concordance* for these lists.

MIRACLES PERFORMED BY CHRIST

MIRACLES	MATT.	MARK	LUKE	JOHN
1. *Narrated in one Gospel only*				
Two Blind Men Healed	9:27			
A Dumb Demoniac Healed	9:32			
Stater in the Mouth of the Fish	17:24			
The Deaf and Dumb Man Healed		7:31		
A Blind Man Healed		8:22		
When Christ Passed Unseen Through the Multitude			4:30	
Draught of Fishes			5:1	
Raising the Widow's Son			7:11	
Healing the Crooked Woman			13:11	
Healing the Man with the Dropsy			14:1	
Healing the Ten Lepers			17:11	
Healing the Ear of Malchus, Servant of the High Priest			22:50	
Turning the Water into Wine				2:1
Healing of the Nobleman's Son (of fever)				4:46
Healing of the Impotent Man of Bethesda				5:1
Healing the Man Born Blind				9:1
Raising of Lazarus				11:43
Draught of Fishes				21:1
2. *Narrated in two Gospels*				
Demoniac in Synagogue Cured		1:23	4:33	
Healing Centurion's Servant (of palsy)	8:5		7:1	
The Blind and Dumb Demoniac	12:22		11:14	
Healing the Daughter of the Syrophenician	15:21	7:24		
Feeding the Four Thousand	15:32	8:1		
Cursing the Fig Tree	21:18	11:12		
3. *Narrated in Three Gospels*				
Healing the Leper	8:2	1:40	5:12	
Healing Peter's Mother-in-law	8:14	1:30	4:38	
Stilling the Storm	8:26	4:37	8:22	
The Legion of Devils Entering Swine	8:28	5:1	8:27	
Healing the Man Sick of the Palsy	9:2	2:3	5:18	
Healing Woman with Issue of Blood	9:20	5:25	8:43	
Raising of Jairus' Daughter	9:23	5:38	8:49	
Healing the Man with a Withered Hand	12:10	3:1	6:6	
Walking on the Sea	14:25	6:48		6:19
Curing Demoniac Child	17:14	9:17	9:38	
Curing Blind Bartimaeus (two blind men)	20:30	10:46	18:35	
4. *Narrated in four Gospels*				
Feeding the Five Thousand	14:19	6:35	9:12	6:5

172

PARABLES SPOKEN BY CHRIST

PARABLES	MATT.	MARK	LUKE	LEADING LESSONS
1. Recorded in one Gospel only				
The Tares	13:24			Good and Evil in Life and Judgment.
The Hid Treasure	13:44			Value of the Gospel
The Goodly Pearl	13:45			The Seeker Finding Salvation.
The Draw-net	13:47			Visible Church a Mixed Body.
The Unmerciful Servant	18:23			Duty of Forgiveness.
The Laborers in the Vineyard.	20:1			Precedence in Service Gives No Claim for Priority in Reward.
The Two Sons	21:28			Insincerity and Repentance.
The Marriage of the King's Son	22:2			Necessity of the Robe of Righteousness.
The Ten Virgins	25:1			Watchful Preparation and Careless Security.
The Talents	25:14			Use of Advantages.
The Sheep and Goats	25:31			Love the Test of Life.
The Seed Growing Secretly		4:26		The Law of Growth in Religion.
The Householder		13:34		Watchfulness.
The Two Debtors			7:41	Gratitude for Pardon.
The Good Samaritan			10:30	Active Benevolence.
The Importunate Friend			11:5	Perseverance in Prayer.
The Rich Fool			12:16	Worldly-mindedness.
Servants Watching			12:35	Expectancy of the Second Coming.
The Wise Steward			12:42	Conscientiousness in Trust.
The Barren Fig Tree			13:6	Unprofitableness under Grace.
The Great Supper			14:16	Universality of the Divine Call.
Building Tower—King Going to War			14:28	Prudence and Self-denial.
The Piece of Money			15:8	Joy over Penitence.
The Prodigal Son			15:11	Fatherly Love to Returning Sinner.
The Unjust Steward			16:1	Faithfulness to Trust.
The Rich Man and Lazarus			16:19	Hopeless Future of the Unfaithful.
Unprofitable Servants			17:7	God's Claim on All Our Service.
The Unjust Judge			18:2	Advantage of Persevering Prayer.
The Pharisee and Publican			18:10	Self-righteousness and Humility.
The Pounds			19:12	Diligence Rewarded, Sloth Punished.
2. Recorded in two Gospels				
House on Rock, and on the Sand	7:24		6:47	Consistent and False Profession.
The Leaven	13:33		13:20	Pervading Influence of Religion.
The Lost Sheep	18:12		15:4	Joy over Penitent.

173

PARABLES	MATT.	MARK	LUKE	LEADING LESSONS
3. Recorded in Three Gospels				
Candle under a Bushel.......	5:15	4:21	8:16 11:33	Dissemination of Truth.
New Cloth on Old Garment..	9:16	2:21	5:36	New Doctrine on Old Prejudices.
New Wine in Old Bottles....	9:17	2:22	5:37	New Spirit in Unregenerate Heart.
The Sower	13:3	4:3	8:5	Hearers Divided into Classes.
The Mustard Seed............	13:31	4:30	13:18	Spread of the Gospel.
The Wicked Husbandmen....	21:33	12:1	20:9	Rejection of Christ by the Jews.
The Fig Tree and All the Trees	24:32	13:28	21:29	Indications of Second Advent.

NOTABLE PASSAGES IN THE GOSPELS

In the Gospels and in the other New Testament books the precious passages are so numerous that a comprehensive list would be so long as to defeat its own purpose. For that reason only such brief lists are offered as the student may readily fix in mind. And in order to facilitate the memorizing only the chapter references are given, as a rule.

IN MATTHEW:

Visit of the Wise Men—Matt. 2.
Christ's Temptations—Matt. 4.
Sermon on the Mount—Matt. 5-7.
"Come unto me, all ye that labor"—Matt. 11 (end).
The Sower and Seven Other Parables—Matt. 13.
Peter's Great Confession—Matt. 16.
Christ's Triumphal Entry—Matt. 21.
Ten Virgins, Talents, and Last Judgment—Matt. 25.
The Great Commission—Matt. 28 (end).

IN MARK:

A Cluster of Miracles—Mark 1.
Feeding of the Five Thousand—Mark 6.
The Transfiguration of Jesus—Mark 9.
Jesus Blessing the Children—Mark 10:13-16.
Jesus' Life a Ransom for All—Mark 10:45.

IN LUKE:

The Christmas Gospel—Luke 2.
The Good Samaritan—Luke 10 (middle).
The Great Supper—Luke 14.
Lost Sheep, Lost Coin, and Prodigal Son—Luke 15.

Rich Man and Lazarus—Luke 16 (end).
Pharisee and Publican—Luke 18.

IN JOHN:

Christ the Eternal Word—John 1.
Nicodemus and the Little Gospel—John 3.
The Samaritan Woman—John 4.
Jesus the Bread of Life—John 6.
Jesus the Good Shepherd—John 10.
The Raising of Lazarus—John 11.
The Foot-washing—John 13.
"Let not your heart be troubled"—John 14.
The Vine and the Branches—John 15.
The Promise of the Holy Spirit—John 16.
Christ's High Priestly Prayer—John 17.

IN ALL THE GOSPELS:

Passion, Death, and Resurrection of Christ—Last chapters.

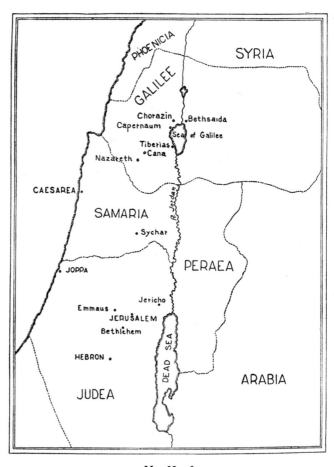

Map No. 6
Palestine in the Time of Christ

176

CHAPTER LV

Acts: The Holy Spirit at Work

NAME.—The full name of this book is *The Acts of the Apostles.*

AUTHOR.—The author is Luke, the physician, who wrote the third Gospel. Luke was a Greek Christian and a companion of Paul.

TIME OF WRITING.—Between 65 and 70 A. D.

PERIOD OF TIME COVERED.—From the ascension of Christ to the imprisonment of Paul in Rome, 30-63 A. D.

NUMBER OF CHAPTERS.—28.

CONTENTS.—The theme and contents of this book are well indicated by verse 8 in chapter 1. "But ye shall receive power, after that the Holy Ghost is come upon you: and ye shall be witnesses unto me, both in Jerusalem, and in all Judaea, and in Samaria, and unto the uttermost part of the earth."

In accordance with this verse the book records the coming of the Holy Spirit, the founding of the Christian Church, and the witnessing of the Apostles, resulting in the wide extension of Christianity among Jews and Gentiles. The book does not record all the work of all the Apostles, by any means. While the activities of other Apostles are referred to, the book deals mainly with the work of the Holy Spirit through the leadership of Peter and Paul.

For the idea of the following outline we are indebted to Dean Samuel M. Miller in his notes on Acts.

OUTLINE OF ACTS

Theme: The Holy Spirit at Work		
In Jerusalem	In Judea and Samaria	Unto the Uttermost Part of the Earth
Chapters 1-7	Chapters 8-12	Chapters 13-28
Church Founded	Church Scattered	Church Extended
Among Jews	Transition from Jews to Gentiles	Among Gentiles
Leader—Peter		Leader—Paul

STUDY SUGGESTIONS

I. THE FIRST SECTION, Chapters 1-7, deals with the promise of and the coming of the Holy Spirit, the founding of the church in Jerusalem, and the experiences of the Apostles and the early Christians up to the martyrdom of Stephen.

Chapter 1.

1. What does a comparison of Acts 1:1-5 with Luke 1:1-4 suggest?

2. What promise did Jesus give? 1:6-8.

3. What statement to the Apostles was made in connection with Christ's Ascension? 1:9-11.

4. What did the Christians do while awaiting the coming of the Holy Spirit? 1:12-14.

5. How was the place of Judas Iscariot in the ranks of the twelve filled? 1:15-26.

Chapter 2.

1. What significant event is recorded in 2:1-4? The name *Pentecost* is derived from a Greek word meaning *fiftieth*. It was the name given to the Jewish festival which came fifty days after the Passover. The name has been continued among Christians to designate the day commemorating the outpouring of the Holy Spirit. Pentecost marks, therefore, the birthday of the Christian Church.

2. What impression did the event produce? 2:5-13.

3. What are the main ideas in Peter's sermon? 2:14-36.

4. What effect did it have? 2:37-41.

5. What attractive picture of the early church is presented in 2:42-47?

Chapter 3.

1. What notable facts are stated in the account of the healing of the lame man? 3:1-10.

178

2. How does Peter account for the healing? 3:11-26.

3. What recurring idea do you note in verses 18, 22, 24 and 25?

Chapter 4.

1. How did the preaching of the Apostles affect the leaders of the Jews? 4:1-3.

2. What do you note in 4:4?

3. How does Peter's conduct, as recorded in 4:5-12, compare with his former denial of Christ? What had happened in the meantime?

4. What impression on the Jewish leaders did the Apostles produce? 4:13-14.

5. How did they attempt to stop the work of the Apostles? 4:15-22.

6. How did the Apostles regard their trials? 4:23-31.

7. What does 4:32-37 tell us about the early Christians?

Chapter 5.

1. Why were Ananias and Sapphira so severely punished? 5:1-11.

2. What remarkable facts are recorded in 5:12-16?

3. What answer did Peter and the other Apostles make at their second trial by the council? 5:17-32.

4. Why, do you think, did Gamaliel give the advice that he did? 5:33-40.

5. What do you note in 5:41-42?

Chapter 6.

1. What division of labor was arranged for in the early church? 6:1-7.

2. By what was Stephen distinguished? 6:8-10.

3. What did his opponents do to him? 6:11-15.

Chapter 7.

1. What was Stephen's object in reviewing the history of Israel? 7:1-53. Note especially verses 51-53.

2. Describe Stephen's martyrdom. 7:54-60.

II. The second section of Acts, Chapters 8-12, records the scattering of the Christians following the persecution in Jerusalem, work in Samaria, the conversion of Saul, Peter's ministries, the conversion of Cornelius, and the persecution by Herod.

Chapter 8.

1. What do you note in 8:1-8?

2. What impression of Simon do you get? 8:9-25.

3. How was the Ethiopian eunuch brought to faith? 8:26-40.

4. What recurring fact do you note in verses 26, 29, and 39?

Chapter 9.

1. What was remarkable about Saul's conversion? 9:1-19.

179

2. What were the immediate effects of his conversion? 9:20-30.
3. What miracles were wrought by Peter? 9:31-43.

Chapter 10.

1. Who was Cornelius? 10:1-2.
2. What vision did he have? 10:3-8.
3. What was the significance of Peter's vision and the events that followed it? 10:9-48.

Chapter 11.

1. How was Peter's action received by the church in Jerusalem? 11:1-18.
2. How widely were the Christians scattered? 11:19-26.
3. What interesting facts are recorded in 11:25-26?
4. What evidence of a Christian spirit is revealed in 11:27-30?

Chapter 12.

1. What trial did the church meet with? 12:1-3.
2. How was Peter's life saved? 12:4-17.
3. How did Herod's life end? 12:18-23.
4. Why is 12:24 a significant verse?

III. THE THIRD SECTION OF ACTS, Chapters 13-28, records Paul's three missionary journeys, a church council in Jerusalem, Paul's imprisonment, trials, and journey to Rome.

Chapter 13.

1. How were the first missionaries selected and ordained? 13:1-3.
2. Note the course of the *first missionary journey* on the map, page 181. 13:4 ff.
3. What obstacle in the work was encountered at Paphos? 13:4-12.
4. What do you note in 13:9?
5. What is stated about John in 13:13? Cf. 12:25 and 13:5.
6. What experiences did the missionaries meet with in Antioch of Pisidia? 13:14-52.
Paul's sermon at Antioch is very interesting as throwing light on his method of presenting the Christian message. What, in brief, was his method?

Chapter 14.

1. How were the missionaries received in Iconium? 14:1-7.
2. What curious experience did they have at Lystra? 14:8-18.
3. How was Paul treated at Lystra? 14:19-20.
4. What was done on the return journey? 14:21-26.
5. What report did the missionaries give on their return to Antioch in Syria? 14:27-28. This was probably the first Christian missionary festival in history.

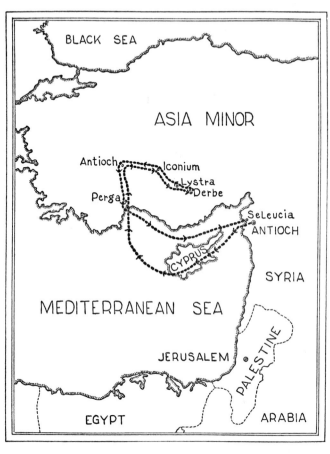

BLACK SEA

ASIA MINOR

Antioch — Iconium
— Lystra
Derbe
Perga
Seleucia
ANTIOCH

CYPRUS

SYRIA

MEDITERRANEAN SEA

PALESTINE

JERUSALEM

EGYPT

ARABIA

Map No. 7
Paul's First Missionary Journey

181

Chapter 15.

1. What was the occasion for the church council in Jerusalem? 15:1-12.

2. What was the decision of the council? 15:13-29.

3. How was the decision received by the Christians at Antioch? 15:30-35.

Note on the decision of the Jerusalem council.— The decision of this council was extremely significant. If circumcision and conformity to the Jewish ceremonial laws had been required of Christians, the Christian religion would have been regarded as a sect of Judaism and could not have become a religion of universal appeal. As it was, the decision set Christianity free from such hampering limitations.

4. What unpleasantness is recorded in 15:36-41? What resulted from it?

Chapter 16.

1. Note the course of the *second missionary journey* on the map, page 183.

2. Who was added to the missionary group at Lystra? 16:1-3.

3. What message did the missionaries deliver on their way? 16:4-5.

4. How were the missionaries guided in their course? 16:6-12.

5. Note the introduction of the pronoun *we* in 16:10. What is the significance of this?

6. Who was the first European convert to Christianity? 16:13-15.

7. What episodes occurred in Philippi as described in 16:16-40?

8. Comment on v. 25.

9. What does the jailor's question reveal? V. 30. Note Paul's answer.

10. What evidences did the jailor give of the reality of his conversion? 16:33-34.

11. Why did Paul make the demand recorded in 16:37?

Chapter 17.

1. What experiences are repeated in Thessalonica? 17:1-9.

2. What do you note in v. 6b?

3. How do the Jews in Thessalonica and Berea compare? 17:10-15.

4. What led up to Paul's address at Athens? 17:16-21.

5. What is the main idea of his address? 17:22-31.

6. What effect did it have? 17:32-33.

Chapter 18.

1. How did Paul make his living in Corinth? 18:1-3.

Map No. 8
Paul's Second Missionary Journey

183

2. What attitude did the Jews take in this city? 18:4-17.

3. Note the brief visit to Ephesus and the promise to return. 18:18-21.

4. The church referred to in 18:22 was apparently the one at Jerusalem.

5. The start of the *third missionary journey* is recorded in 18:23.

6. Note the course of the *third missionary journey* on the map, page 185.

7. What is said about Apollos in 18:24-28?

Chapter 19.

1. What was peculiar about the disciples Paul found at Ephesus? 19:1-7.

2. What events in 19:8-41 show the growth of the influence of the Gospel?

Chapter 20.

1. What event occurred at Troas? 20:7-12.

2. What light does Paul's address to the Ephesian elders throw upon him as a shepherd of souls? 20:17-38.

Chapter 21.

1. What warnings did Paul receive on the way to Jerusalem? 21:1-16.

2. What action did he agree to at the request of Christians in Jerusalem? 21:17-26.

3. What was the cause of the bitter hostility to him on the part of the Jews? 21:27-36.

4. How was his Roman citizenship useful to him? 21:37-40

Chapter 22.

1. What is the main content of Paul's address? 22:1-21.

2. Why was he not permitted to complete his defense? 22:22.

3. What use did he again make of his Roman citizenship? 22:23-30.

Chapter 23.

1. Did Paul lose his temper before the council? 23:1-5.

2. What caused the disruption of the council? 23:6-10.

3. What do you note in 23:11?

4. What plot against Paul was made? 23:12-15.

5. How was he rescued? 23:16-35.

Chapter 24.

1. What charges against Paul did Tertullus bring? 24:1-9.

2. How did Paul meet these charges? 24:10-21.

3. What effect did Paul's speaking have upon Felix? 24:22-25.

4. What do you note in 24:26?

5. How long was Paul imprisoned in Caesarea? 24:27.

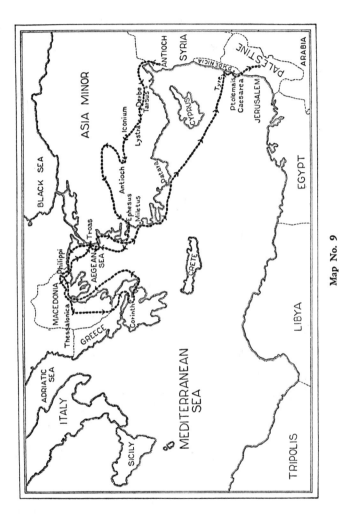

Map No. 9
Paul's Third Missionary Journey

Chapter 25.

1. What right as a Roman citizen did Paul make use of? 25:1-12.
2. What was Festus' purpose in bringing Paul before Agrippa? 25:13-27.

Chapter 26.

1. What is the main content of Paul's address before Agrippa? 26:1-23.
2. How was Agrippa affected? 26:24-29.
3. What do you note in a comparison of 26:28-29 with 24:25?
4. What was Agrippa's judgment concerning Paul? 26:30-32.

Chapter 27.

1. Note the course of Paul's voyage to Rome, on the map, page 187.
2. List the items of especial interest in connection with this voyage? Chapter 27.
3. How does Paul's natural aptitude for leadership appear?

Chapter 28.

1. What items of interest do you note in connection with the stay on the island of Melita? 28:1-7.
2. How was Paul received in Rome by the Christians, by the Roman authorities, and by the Jews? 28:8-28.
3. How does the book of *Acts* leave Paul? 28:30-31.

NOTE ON THE LATER CAREER OF PAUL.—According to passages in the Epistles and tradition Paul was released from his first imprisonment in Rome in 63 A. D. He continued his missionary labors, revisiting his churches in the East, and probably went westward as far as Spain. Finally he was again arrested and imprisoned in Rome, and during the persecution under Nero was beheaded there in 67 A. D.

ADDITIONAL STUDY SUGGESTIONS

1. Note the influence and activity of the Holy Spirit as recorded in *Acts*.
2. Make a study of the expansion of Christianity.
3. Make a study of the Missionary Journeys of Paul. See the maps.
4. Make a study of the character and career of Peter.
5. Do the same for Paul.

NOTABLE PASSAGES IN ACTS

The Ascension of Jesus, Chapter 1. Pentecost, Chapter 2. Paul's Conversion, Chapter 9. The Jerusalem Council, Chapter 15. The Conversion of the Philippian Jailor, Chapter 16. Paul's Address at Athens, Chapter 17.

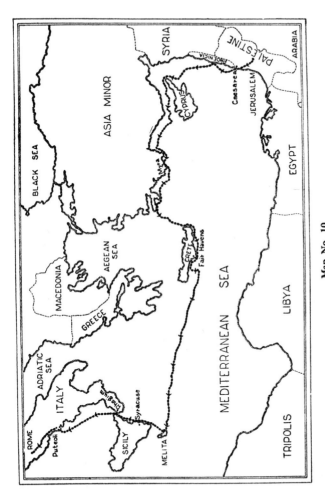

Map No. 10
Paul's Voyage to Rome

187

CHAPTER LVI

The Epistles

Of the 27 books in the New Testament 21 are in the form of letters to individuals, churches, or Christians in general. The name *epistle* is from the Latin word *epistola,* which means *letter.*

The Epistles contain fruits of reflection on the facts of Christ's life, work, teachings, sufferings, death, resurrection and ascension, and constitute our main sources of knowledge of such Christian doctrines as the Trinity, the person of Christ, the nature of man, Christ's relations to the human race and to the church, the Atonement, justification by faith, sanctification by the Holy Spirit, and the last things.

These letters of the Apostles, furthermore, contain a wealth of instructions, advice, and admonitions regarding the life and conduct of Christians, and constitute therefore extremely valuable treatises on Christian ethics.

They also give a very vivid impression of the conditions of the early Christians and of the personal circumstances of the writers. They afford us glimpses of the life as it was actually lived at that time.

THE EPISTLES OF PAUL

The first thirteen Epistles are by the Apostle Paul. They were written after Paul was about 50 years of age and give, therefore, his mature, Spirit-guided thought on a variety of subjects.

We may group in tabular form a number of significant facts relating to Paul's Epistles in the order in which they were written, as follows:

Group	Paul's Circumstances	Theme of Group	Name of Epistle	No. of Chapters	Sent from	Date
1	On Second Missionary Journey	Christ's Second Coming	I Thes.	5	Corinth	52
			II Thes.	3	Corinth (?)	53
2	On Third Missionary Journey	Anti-Judaic (Controversial)	I Cor.	16	Ephesus	57
			II Cor.	13	Philippi (?)	58
			Galatians	6	Corinth	58
			Romans	16	Corinth	58
3	First Imprisonment at Rome	Christological and Personal	Phil.	4	Rome	62
			Col.	4	Rome	63
			Philemon	1	Rome	63
			Ephesians	6	Rome	63
4	Paul's Last Years	Pastoral	I Tim.	6	Macedonia (?)	66 (?)
			Titus	3	Macedonia (?)	66 (?)
			II Tim.	4	Rome	67 (?)

The present order of the Epistles of Paul in the New Testament is not chronological, however. The order there seems to have been determined by the relative length or importance of the letters. It is as follows:

> Romans
> I Corinthians
> II Corinthians
> Galatians
> Ephesians
> Philippians
> Colossians
> I Thessalonians
> II Thessalonians
> I Timothy
> II Timothy
> Titus
> Philemon

It will assist in reading and studying the Epistles to bear in mind that they are usually cast in the following form:

1. Salutation and statement of subject.

2. Thanksgiving for the Christian faith and conduct of those addressed.

3. A doctrinal section.

189

4. A section of practical applications of the truths discussed.
   5. Personal matters, messages, greetings, etc.
   6. A conclusion in Paul's own hand as evidence of authenticity.

This survey does not attempt any extended study of the Epistles. We must content ourselves with a brief statement of the occasion of each letter, an outline of the contents, study suggestions, and reference to especially notable passages. The order of the books in the New Testament is followed.

CHAPTER LVII

Romans: Justification by Faith

OCCASION.—There was a Christian congregation in Rome, composed of converted Jews and Gentiles. The church there had probably been founded by visitors in Jerusalem at the time of the miracle of Pentecost, who had accepted the Christian faith there. Paul had for a long time desired to go to Rome, and so when the possibility of his going there seemed likely he wrote this letter to prepare the Roman Christians for his coming and possibly to correct certain misrepresentations of his religious position which had reached them. The Epistle sets forth at considerable length the heart of the Christian message —Justification by faith in the atoning merits of Jesus Christ.

OUTLINE OF ROMANS

Theme: Justification by Faith in Christ						
Introduction		Doctrinal			Practical	
1:1-15		1:16—11:36			12-16	
Salu-tation 1:1-7	Thanks-giving 1:8-15 Theme Stated 1:16-17	Univer-sality of Sin 1:18–3:20	Univer-sality of Grace 3:21–8:39	Apparent Rejection of Israel 9-11	Chris-tian Duties 12:1 15:13	Personal Matters Etc. 15:14 16:27

STUDY SUGGESTIONS

I. SALUTATION. Chapter 1:1-7.
1. What facts about himself does Paul give in this salutation?
2. What facts does he state about Jesus Christ?
3. To whom is the letter addressed?
4. What does he wish for his readers? V. 7.

II. THANKSGIVING. Chapter 1:8-15.
1. What is Paul grateful for?
2. What earnest desire does he reveal?

191

III. STATEMENT OF THEME. Chapter 1:16-17.

1. In what different ways is the theme of the letter expressed?
2. Note that the statement, "The righteous shall live by faith," is a quotation from Habakkuk 2:4.

IV. THE UNIVERSALITY OF SIN. Chapters 1:18—3:20.

A. *The guilt of the Gentiles.* 1:18-32.
1. What cause is given in 18-23 for the unrighteousness of the Gentiles?
2. What are some of the chief sins of which they became guilty? 24-32.
B. *The guilt of the Jews.* 2:1—3:8.
1. Why are the Jews also guilty before God? 2:1-16. Note especially v. 13.
2. Why is the guilt of the Jews in a sense even greater than that of the Gentiles? 2:17—3:8.
C. *The guilt of all.* 3:9-20.
1. The arraignment of the guilt of all mankind, 10-18, is made up of quotations from various books in the Old Testament as indicated in the marginal notes.
2. What universal statement is made in v. 20?

V. THE UNIVERSALITY OF GRACE. Chapters 3:21—8:39.

A. *Salvation by grace through faith in Christ.* 3:21-31.
1. What way of salvation is pointed out in 3:21-31?
2. What is stated about this way in the last part of v. 21?
B. *The place of faith in Old Testament times.* Chapter 4.
1. What is said about Abraham? 1-5.
2. What is said about David? 6-8.
3. What is the relationship between faith and circumcision? 9-12.
4. What is the relationship between faith and the law? 13-18.
5. How does the case of Abraham apply to other believers? 19-25.
C. *The grounds of confidence for all believers.* Chapter 5.
1. What blessed truth is stated in 5:1?
2. To what qualities and acts of God is our salvation due? 1-11. Note especially v. 8.
3. What is the difference between Adam and Christ in relation to men? 5:12-21.
D. *Relation between faith and morality.* 6:1—8:17.
1. What wrong idea does Paul combat in Chapter 6?
2. What inward conflict is pictured in Chapter 7?
3. How is the Christian a free being? 8:1-17.
E. *The glorious hope of the Christian.* 8:18-39.
1. To what may the Christian hopefully look forward? 18-25.
2. How is the Spirit helpful? 26-30.
3. What abiding confidence may Christians have? 31-39.

VI. The Relation of the Jews to the Doctrine of the Universality of Grace. Chapters 9-11.

1. What deep concern for his people does Paul reveal? 9:1-5.
2. How does Paul show that the failure of the Jews to believe is not due to deficiencies in God? 9:6-33.
3. What do you note in 9:31-33?
4. What is the real reason for the rejection of Christ by the Jews? Chapter 10.
5. How does Paul show that the Jews have not been totally rejected? 11:1-24.
6. What prospect is held out in 25-32?
7. Note Paul's admiration for the unsearchable wisdom of God. 33-36.

VII. Practical Section—Ideals for the Christian Life. Chapters 12:1—15:13.

1. Chapter 12 sets forth a beautiful program for the Christian life. It sounds like an echo of Jesus' "Sermon on the Mount."
2. What ideal of consecration is set forth in 12:1?
3. Make a list of the chief Christian virtues extolled in Chapter 12.
4. What principles of citizenship are enumerated in 13:1-7?
5. Summarize 13:8-9 in a single word.
6. Do the same for 13:11-14.
7. What fundamental Christian attitude is discussed in Chapter 14?
8. What should be the Christian's model of conduct? 15:1-13.

VIII. Personal Matters and Greetings. Chapters 15:14—16:27.

1. What does Paul consider his chief mission in life to be, according to 15:14-22?
2. What personal plans does Paul outline in 15:22-29?
3. What request does he make? 15:30-33.
4. What impression of Paul do you get from the long list of persons mentioned by name in 16:1-21?
5. What type of people does Paul warn against in 16:17-20?
6. Note that Tertius served as Paul's secretary in writing the letter. 16:22.
7. Note the concluding doxology, 16:25-27.

Notable Passages in Romans

Rom. 1:16—The Power of the Gospel. Rom. 5—Justification by faith in Christ. Rom. 12—Christian ideals.

CHAPTER LVIII

I Corinthians: Church Discipline

OCCASION.—Paul founded the church in Corinth, in 52 A. D., on his second missionary journey. Some time afterward strife arose among four different parties in the church, and very serious moral disorders also developed. Reports of this sad state of affairs reached Paul, and he wrote this epistle to try to put a stop to the disorders. The Epistle deals, therefore, with church discipline.

OUTLINE OF I CORINTHIANS

Theme: Correction of Disorders in the Church						
Salutation and Thanksgiving Chapter 1:1-9	The Party Spirit Chapters 1:10—4:21	Moral Disorders Chapters 5-6	Abuse of Christian Freedom Chapters 7-10	Disorders in Worship Chapters 11-14	Instruction Regarding the Resurrection Chapter 15	Admonitions and Greetings Chapter 16

STUDY SUGGESTIONS

I. INTRODUCTION. Chapter 1:1-9.

1. From whom is the letter sent? 1:1.
2. To whom is the letter sent? 1:2.
3. For what is Paul thankful? 1:4-9.

II. THE PARTY SPIRIT. Chapters 1:10—4:21.

1. How many parties were there in the Corinthian church? 1:10-17.
2. What types of wisdom are contrasted in 1:18-31?
3. Why was the cross a stumbling-block to the Jews and foolishness to the Gentiles?
4. What method of preaching had Paul used at Corinth? 2:1-5.
5. How only can men learn to understand the mysteries of God? 2:6-16.
6. Why did Paul have to deal with the people at Corinth as babes? 3:1-9.
7. How did Paul look upon his work at Corinth? 3:10-15.
8. Instead of glorying in men, what should the Corinthians do? 3:16-23.

9. What contrast does Paul set forth between the spirit of the Apostles and the spirit of the Corinthians? Chapter 4.

III. Moral Disorders. Chapters 5-6.

1. How ought the Christians to deal with moral lapses among themselves? Chapter 5.

2. Instead of going to law with one another how ought disputes to be settled? 6:1-8.

3. What solemn warning does Paul give? 6:9-11.

4. What view of the body tends to moral purity? 6:12-20.

IV. Abuse of Christian Freedom. Chapters 7-10.

1. What views on marriage did Paul hold? Chapter 7.

2. What principle should govern in the matter of eating meat that had been presented before idols? Chapter 8.

3. What attitude did Paul take to his apostolic liberty? Chapter 9.

4. What lessons does Paul derive from the history of Israel as to idolatrous practices? Chapter 10.

V. Disorders in Worship. Chapters 11-14.

1. What is Paul's view of woman's apparel in church? 11:2-16.

2. What disorders connected with the Lord's Supper does Paul warn against? 11:17-34.

3. What is the relationship that should exist among Christians with different gifts and aptitudes? Chapter 12.

4. What is the greatest of all Christian virtues? Chapter 13.

5. What instructions regarding the gift of tongues does Paul give? Chapter 14.

VI. Instruction Regarding the Resurrection. Chapter 15.

1. What evidences for the resurrection of Christ does Paul present? 15:1-11.

2. What is the significance of Christ's resurrection? 15:12-34.

3. What is to be the nature of the resurrected bodies? 15:35-58.

VII. Conclusion. Personal Matters and Greetings. Chapter 16.

1. What personal plans does Paul speak of? 16:1-12.

2. What are his final admonitions? 16:13-16.

3. Note Paul's gracious acknowledgments and friendly greetings. 16:17-24.

Notable Passages in I Corinthians

Spiritual Wisdom, Chapter 2. Love the Greatest Quality, Chapter 13. The Resurrection of Christ and Believers, Chapter 15.

CHAPTER LIX

II Corinthians: Defense of Church Discipline

OCCASION.—Paul's first letter to the Corinthians brought about fairly good results, for which Paul was grateful. But reports came to him that his authority as an Apostle and his right to exercise discipline was being questioned. In his second letter he deals, therefore, with these matters.

OUTLINE OF II CORINTHIANS

Theme: Defense of Paul's Disciplinary Authority				
Salutation and Thanksgiving 1:1-11	Defense of His Ministry 1:12–7:16	Defense of Collection for the Poor 8-9	Defense of His Authority 10-12	Admonition and Greetings 13

STUDY SUGGESTIONS

I. INTRODUCTION. Chapter 1:1-11.

1. From whom and to whom was this letter sent? 1:1-3.
2. How did Paul look upon hi. hardships? 1:3-11.

II. PAUL'S DEFENSE OF HIS MINISTRY. Chapters 1:12—7:16.

1. In what spirit had Paul conducted his work among the Corinthians? 1:12-14.
2. Why had Paul written to them instead of going to visit them in person? 1:15—2:4.
3. What attitude does Paul urge toward the man who had been disciplined? 2:5-11.
4. How had God blessed Paul's ministry in Macedonia? 2:12-17.
5. What excellencies does Paul claim for his new covenant ministry? Chapter 3.
6. In spite of affliction and persecution, how had Paul glorified God through his ministry? Chapter 4.
7. With what confidence and in what spirit had Paul labored? Chapter 5.

8. What was the heart of Paul's ministry of reconciliation? 5:18-19.

NOTE.—Verse 19 epitomizes in a wonderful way the essence of the Christian Gospel. It makes clear:

a) That God took the initiative in bringing men back into fellowship with Himself.
b) That Christ is true God.
c) That the redemptive process worked through Christ.
d) That sins are forgiven for Christ's sake.
e) That the proclamation of this reconciliation is the work of Christian ministers.

9. How does Paul demonstrate the earnestness and sincerity of his ministry? 6:1-11.

10. What in turn does he expect of the Corinthians? 6:12-18.

11. According to the report by Titus, what effect had Paul's first letter to the Corinthians had? Chapter 7.

III. COLLECTION FOR THE POOR. Chapters 8-9.

1. In his efforts to collect money for the poor in Jerusalem, how does Paul motivate his appeal? Chapter 8.

2. What reflex blessings would the Corinthians experience for their liberality? Chapter 9.

IV. PAUL'S DEFENSE OF HIS AUTHORITY. Chapters 10-12.

1. How does Paul meet the charge of the critics that he was weak? Chapter 10.

2. What commendation of himself does he feel forced to make? Chapter 11.

3. What wonderful experience does Paul relate? 12:1-4.

4. What was the purpose of the thorn in the flesh? 12:5-10.

5. What was Paul's fundamental purpose in dealing with the Corinthians? 12:11-21.

V. CONCLUSION. Chapter 13.

1. In what spirit is Paul contemplating a visit to Corinth? 13:1-10.

2. Note the admonition and the beautiful promise in 13:11.

3. Note the complete form of the Apostolic Benediction in 13:14.

NOTABLE PASSAGES IN II CORINTHIANS

The Christian a New Creature, Chapter 5. The "Thorn in the Flesh," Chapter 12.

CHAPTER LX

Galatians: Justification by Faith, Not Law

OCCASION.—Paul founded churches in Galatia on his second missionary journey, and revisited them on his third journey. Later, while at Corinth, he heard that certain agitators called Judaists were misleading the Galatian Christians, contending that Paul was no real Apostle and that in order to be saved they must conform to the Jewish ceremonial law, including circumcision. In this letter Paul defends his apostolic authority and re-emphasizes the true evangelical doctrine that salvation is by grace, not by law.

The emphatic presentation of the doctrine of justification by faith in this Epistle has throughout history served most effectively to offset the deadening influence of all forms of legalism and externalism in Christianity. It was greatly favored and much used by Luther and other Reformation leaders.

OUTLINE OF GALATIANS

Theme: Justification by Faith, Not By Law				
Greeting and Occasion for Writing 1:1-10	Paul's Defense of His Apostolic Authority 1:11–2:21	Argument for Justification by Faith 3-4	Right Use of Christian Liberty 5:1–6:10	Summary and Benediction 6:11-18

STUDY SUGGESTIONS

I. SALUTATION AND OCCASION FOR WRITING. Chapter 1:1-10.

1. To whom does Paul attribute his apostleship in Verse 1?
2. What situation among the Galatians is alluded to in 1:6-10?

II. Paul's Defense of His Apostleship. Chapters 1:11—2:21.

1. In establishing the proposition that he was a true Apostle what facts does Paul set forth in 1:11—2:10?
2. What specific exercise of his apostolic office does he refer to in 2:11-21?

III. Argument for Justification by Faith. Chapters 3-4.

1. What foolishness on the part of the Galatians does Paul criticize? 3:1-5.
2. On what grounds did blessings come to Abraham and the spiritual sons of Abraham? 3:6-14.
3. If justification is by faith, what is the purpose of the law? 3:15-29.
4. Under what figures does Paul compare the state of men before and after coming into right relationship with Christ? 4:1-11.
5. What deep concern does Paul manifest? 4:12-20.
6. What allegorical lessons does Paul draw from the differences in status between the two sons of Abraham? 4:21-31.

IV. Practical—The Right Use of Christian Liberty. Chapters 5:1—6:10.

1. How did the teachings of the false leaders tend to destroy Christian freedom? 5:1-12.
2. What warning as to the abuse of Christian liberty does Paul give? 5:13-15.
3. What are the fruits of the flesh and the fruits of the Spirit? 5:16-26.
4. What special Christian virtues are urged in 6:1-10?

V. Summary and Benediction. Chapter 6:11-18.

1. What do you note in 6:11? This statement has led many people to believe that Paul had an eye disease which interfered with his sight.
2. Note the brief summary of the letter in 6:12-16.
3. How do you interpret Verse 17?

Notable Passages in Galatians

Justification by Faith, Chapter 3. Christian Liberty, Chapter 5.

CHAPTER LXI

Ephesians: The Church of Christ

Occasion.—When Paul was a prisoner in Rome representatives from various churches came to visit him. Among them was Tychicus from Ephesus. Paul made use of the opportunity to send back with him this beautiful letter in which he sets forth his meditations on the church as the body of Christ. On account of its exalted character in thought and style it has been called the "Alps of the New Testament."

Outline of Ephesians

Theme: The Church of Christ			
Salutation 1:1-2	Doctrinal: The Nature of the Church 1:3–3:21	Practical: Life in the Church 4:1–6:20	Conclusion and Benediction 6:21-24

STUDY SUGGESTIONS

I. Salutation. Chapter 1:1-2.

1. Note again Paul's emphasis upon his apostleship, Verse 1.
2. To whom is the letter addressed?

II. Doctrinal: The Nature of the Christian Church as the Body of Christ. Chapters 1:3—3:21.

A. *The blessings of salvation.* 1:3-14.

1. Note how Paul emphasizes the truth that our salvation is dependent upon Christ. 1:3-14.
2. How many times does "in Christ" or similar expressions occur in 1:3-14?

B. *Prayer for the Christians.* 1:15-23.

1. What ideal development of Christians does Paul pray for? 1:15-23.
2. What relationship exists between Christ and His Church? 1:22-23.

200

C. *The nature of the Church.* Chapters 2-3.

1. In what condition were the members of the church originally? 2:1-10.
2. What had God done with them? 2:1-10.
3. What union had been brought about? 2:11-22.
4. What do you learn about the nature of the Christian church from its comparison with a temple? 2:19-22.
5. What mystery had been revealed to Paul? 3:1-13.
6. What is the central idea in Paul's prayer for the Christians? 3:14-19.
7. What confidence in the power of God is expressed in the doxology? Verses 20-21.

III. Practical. The Life of the Church. Chapters 4:1—6:20.

A. *Exhortation to unity.* 4:1-16.

1. What ideal of unity is set forth in 4:1-6?
2. How may there be unity in diversity? 4:7-16.

B. *Warnings against the vices of heathenism.* 4:17—5:21.

1. What chief classes of sins are warned against in this section? 4:17—5:21.
2. What should be the Christians' model? 5:1-2.

C. *Admonitions as to family and social relationships.* 5:22—6:9.

1. What is the ideal relationship between husband and wife? 5:22-23.
2. Between parents and children? 6:1-4.
3. Between employers and employees? 6:5-9.

D. *Final admonition as to Christian warfare.* 6:10-20.

1. In terms of what striking figure is the Christian life pictured? 6:10-20.
2. What prayer does Paul ask for himself? 6:19-20.

IV. Conclusion and Benediction. Chapter 6:21-24.

1. With what commission was Tychicus entrusted? 6:21-22. Evidently Tychicus was the bearer of the letter.
2. What does Paul wish for his readers? 6:23-24.

Notable Passages in Ephesians

Life Through Christ, Chapter 2. The Stature of the Fulness of Christ, Chapter 4. The Armor of God, Chapter 6.

CHAPTER LXII

Philippians: Christian Joy

OCCASION.—This Epistle is a "thank-you" letter. The church at Philippi had sent a gift to Paul while he was a prisoner in Rome. When the bearer, Epaphroditus, returned, Paul sent this letter with him. He expresses with deep emotion his appreciation of the thoughtfulness of the Philippian Christians and gives them a glimpse into his own heart and life. In spite of his hardships he is jubilantly happy in his fellowship with Christ and fellow Christians. The letter gives us an impressive picture of the human and gracious phase of Paul's character.

OUTLINE OF PHILIPPIANS

Theme: Christian Joy			
Salutation	Joy in the Fellowship of the Gospel	Joy in the Lord	Greetings and Benediction
1:1-2	1:3–2:30	3:1–4:20	4:21-23

STUDY SUGGESTIONS

I. SALUTATION. Chapter 1:1-2.

1. From whom are greetings sent? Verse 1.
2. Who are addressed? Verse 1.

II. JOY IN THE FELLOWSHIP OF THE GOSPEL. Chapters 1:3—2:30.

1. What does Paul thank God for in relation to the Philippians? 1:3-7.
2. What does he pray for? 1:8-11.
3. What hardships and trials does Paul allude to in 1:12-30?
4. Instead of giving way to a spirit of defeatism because of these experiences, what attitude was Paul, by the grace of God, able to maintain?
5. How could the Philippian Christians bring joy to Paul? 2:1-18.

6. Note the remarkable summary of Christ's nature and redemptive work in 2:5-11.

7. In what way did Paul hope to make use of his young friend Timothy? 2:19-24.

8. What is said about Epaphroditus? 2:25-30. See note above on the occasion for the writing of this letter.

III. Joy in the Lord. Chapters 3:1—4:20.

1. What idea recurs in the following verses: 3:1; 4:4; 4:10?

2. Instead of glorying in race, family, and law righteousness, what does Paul glory in? 3:1-11.

3. What is Paul's basic ambition for himself and other Christians? 3:12—4:3.

4. How may enduring joy and peace be had? 4:4-7.

5. Note the beautiful statement of Christian ideals in 4:8-9.

6. How does Paul express his appreciation of the gift sent him? 4:10-20.

IV. Greetings and Benediction. Chapter 4:21-23.

1. Note the all-inclusiveness of the salutation.

2. What does Verse 22 suggest as to the influence of the Gospel in Rome?

Notable Passages in Philippians

The Mind of Christ, Chapter 2. The Excellency of the Knowl edge of Christ, Chapter 3. "Think on these things," Chapter 4:8.

CHAPTER LXIII

Colossians: The Sufficiency of Christ

OCCASION.—The Colossian church was being threatened by false teaching, later known as Gnosticism, a mixture of Jewish legalism and heathen philosophy. This teaching, among other things, challenged the supremacy of Christ and the sufficiency of His merit for salvation. When knowledge of this state of affairs reached Paul in Rome, he wrote this letter in which he eloquently sets forth the preeminence of Christ and the only ground of salvation in Him.

OUTLINE OF COLOSSIANS

Theme: The Sufficiency of Christ			
Salutation, Thanksgiving, and Prayer 1:1-13	Christ as the Object of Faith 1:14–2:23	Christ as the Source of Life 3:1–4:1	Exhortations, Greetings, and Benediction 4:2-18

STUDY SUGGESTIONS

I. INTRODUCTION. Chapter 1:1-13.

1. From whom and to whom was the letter sent? 1:1-2.

2. Notice the mingling of thanksgiving and intercession in Paul's introduction to his letter. 1:3-13.

3. Make a list of the things Paul prays for. 1:3-13.

II. THE SUFFICIENCY OF CHRIST AS THE OBJECT OF FAITH. Chapters 1:14—2:23.

1. How does Paul set forth the preeminence of Christ in 1:14-20?

2. What relationship between believers and Christ did Paul labor to bring about? 1:21-29.

3. What is Paul's constant concern for believers? 2:1-7.

4. What dangers from the side of Gentile philosophy and Jewish legalism does he warn against? 2:8-23.

III. The Sufficiency of Christ as the Source of Life. Chapters 3:1—4:1.

1. What fundamental difference in life ideals does Paul set forth in 3:1-17?

2. What specific application of the law of love does he make in 3:18—4:1?

IV. Conclusion. Chapter 4:2-18.

1. What intercession does Paul ask for? 4:2-4.

2. Note the gracious way in which Paul refers to faithful friends and fellow-workers. He is a fine example of the Christian gentleman. 4:5-18.

Notable Passages in Colossians

The Fullness of the Godhead in Christ, Chapter 2. Putting Off the Old and Putting on the New, Chapter 3.

CHAPTER LXIV

I Thessalonians: The Second Advent

OCCASION.—The church in Thessalonia was founded during the short period of three weeks which Paul spent there on his second missionary journey. He had to leave on account of the hostility of the unbelieving Jews who continued to persecute the Christians. Paul was greatly concerned about them and sent Timothy to comfort and instruct them. Timothy brought back a good report about their faith in the midst of persecution, but also reported that they had misunderstood Paul's teaching about the second coming of Christ and were greatly troubled about those of their loved ones who had died before Christ's return. Paul, therefore, wrote this letter to comfort them in their trials, and to instruct them regarding the manner of the Second Advent. This letter is thought to be the earliest of all the New Testament writings.

OUTLINE OF I THESSALONIANS

Theme: The Second Coming of Christ			
Salutation and Thanksgiving Chapter 1	Paul's Past and Present Concern for the Church Chapters 2-3	Instruction Especially Regarding the Second Advent Chapters 4:1–5:25	Greetings and Benediction Chapter 5:26-28

STUDY SUGGESTIONS

I. INTRODUCTION. Chapter 1.

1. What information do you derive from 1:1?
2. What remarkable qualities of the Thessalonians was Paul thankful for? 1:2-10.

II. PAUL'S PAST AND PRESENT CONCERN FOR THE THESSALONIANS. Chapters 2-3.

1. In what manner had Paul preached, and in what manner had the Thessalonians received the Gospel? Chapter 2.

206

2. What continued interest in the church does Paul manifest?
Chapter 3.

III. CHRISTIAN INSTRUCTIONS, ESPECIALLY REGARDING THE SECOND COMING OF CHRIST. Chapters 4:1— 5:25.

1. What virtues does Paul urge in 4:1-12?
2. What comforting assurance does he give regarding the believing dead and Christ's Second Advent? 4:13-18.
3. Since no one knows the time of Christ's return, what admonitions does Paul give? 5:1-11.
4. Note the list of pithy and significant exhortations in 5:12-25. Some of the shortest verses in the Bible are in this section.

IV. CONCLUSION. Chapter 5:26-28.

1. What importance did Paul attach to his own letters?
Verse 27.

NOTABLE PASSAGES IN I THESSALONIANS

The Christians' Blessed Hope, Chapter 4. Sons of Light, Chapter 5.

CHAPTER LXV

II Thessalonians: The Time of the Second Advent

OCCASION.—The first letter to the Thessalonians was productive of good results. But there still persisted erroneous ideas regarding the Second Coming of Christ. Because many of them were convinced that He was returning very soon, they ceased to work at their occupations, and much want and disorder resulted. II Thessalonians was, therefore, written some months after the first to instruct regarding the time of the Second Advent and to urge people to go back to work.

OUTLINE OF II THESSALONIANS

Theme: The Second Coming of Christ			
Salutation and Thanksgiving Chapter 1:1-4	Manner and Time of Christ's Coming Chapters 1:5–2:12	Present Duties Chapters 2:13–3:15	Greetings and Benediction Chapter 3:16-17

STUDY SUGGESTIONS

I. INTRODUCTION. Chapter 1:1-4.

    1. Compare 1:1 with 1 Thessalonians 1:1.

    2. For what virtues does Paul commend the Thessalonians? 1:3-4.

II. THE SECOND COMING OF CHRIST. Chapters 1:5—2:12.

    1. What will take place in connection with Christ's Second Coming? 1:5-12.

    2. What information does Paul give regarding the time of the Second Advent? 2:1-3.

    3. What picture of the anti-Christ does he present? 2:3-12.

III. PRESENT DUTIES. Chapters 2:13—3:15.

1. In the expectation of Christ's return to judgment, what does Paul urge upon his readers? 2:13—3:5.

2. What wrong attitude toward work does he warn against? 3:6-15.

IV. CONCLUSION. Chapter 3:16-18.

1. What precious gift does Paul ask for his readers? 3:16.

2. What is the mark of genuineness in all Paul's epistles? 3:17.

NOTABLE PASSAGE IN II THESSALONIANS

The Anti-Christ, Chapter 2.

CHAPTER LXVI

I Timothy: The Church and the Ministry

OCCASION.—This Epistle of Paul to Timothy is called a "Pastoral Epistle" because at the time of its writing Timothy was pastor, or bishop, of the church in Ephesus, and the letter contains instruction and advice to him in that capacity. The letter was apparently written after Paul's release from his first imprisonment in Rome. Immediately after Paul was freed from prison, he and Timothy went to Ephesus. There Timothy was left as pastor of the church, while Paul moved on to visit other churches and probably wrote this letter from Macedonia.

The position of pastor of the church in Ephesus was a difficult one. Ephesus was a key city in Asia Minor, and the position of the congregation a strategic one. It was composed of many elements, often differing in their ideas about doctrine, morals, church discipline, and the like. Although he had been with Paul in his work for some 14 years, Timothy was still a comparatively young man, and this letter from his older and more experienced friend must have been very welcome to him. Its aim was to instruct Timothy in the conduct of his high office and to encourage him in the midst of the many difficulties attending his work.

OUTLINE OF I TIMOTHY

Theme: The Church and the Ministry			
Salutation Chapter 1:1-2	True Doctrine and Orderly Worship in the Church Chapters 1:3–3:16	Loyalty to the Gospel; Wisdom and Godliness in the Ministry Chapters 4:1–6:21	Benediction Chapter 6:21b

210

STUDY SUGGESTIONS

I. Salutation. Chapter 1:1-2.

1. What do you learn from 1:1-2 about the sender and recipient of this letter?

2. Note that Timothy is the spiritual child of Paul. This fact constituted a precious bond between them.

II. True Doctrine and Orderly Worship in the Church. Chapters 1:3—3:16.

1. What exhortation to Timothy does Paul repeat? 1:3-4.

2. How does he summarize true religion? 1:5.

3. What wrong tendency in the church in Ephesus is pointed out? 1:6-7.

4. Evidently some of the people had wrong ideas about the law. How does Paul correct this? 1:8-11.

5. In 1:11, Paul refers to his ministry. According to 1:12-17, how does he feel about being a minister of the Gospel? How these words of deep appreciation must have heightened Timothy's idea of his own office!

6. Note the solemn warning to sound doctrine and right living. 1:18-20.

7. For whom should intercessory prayer be offered? 2:1-2.

8. How many people are embraced within the saving plans of God? 2:3-7.

9. By whom has salvation been made possible? 2:5-6.

10. How should Christian men and women conduct themselves? 2:8-15.

11. What qualifications should a bishop or pastor possess? 3:1-7. Apparently no distinction had developed at this time between the offices of *bishop* and *pastor.* The word *bishop* comes from a Greek word meaning *overseer.*

12. What sort of people should be chosen as deacons and deaconesses? 3:8-13.

13. What reason does Paul give for writing? 3:14-15.

14. 3:16 is thought to be an ancient Christian hymn. Note how it summarizes the life of Christ.

III. Loyalty to the Gospel; Wisdom and Godliness in the Ministry. Chapters 4:1—6:21.

1. What prophecy does the Spirit utter through Paul? 4:1-5.

2. What responsibility of Timothy is pointed out in this connection? 4:6-11.

3. Enumerate the items of advice given to Timothy. 4:12-16. What a wonderful spiritual father Paul was!

4. What good advice does Paul offer for dealing with both old and young? 5:1-2.

5. What instructions about widows does he give? 5:3-16.

6. How are ruling elders to be treated? 5:17-21.

7. What personal advice does Paul give? 5:22-25. As a spiritual father Paul was deeply concerned about the smallest details of Timothy's life. Though he carried on his heart responsibility for all the churches, he was not too occupied to be interested in individual men. An example for all Christians.

8. What advice to servants is given in 6:1-2? How does this apply to employees at the present time?

9. What does Paul warn against? 6:3-10. What may we learn from this?

10. What stirring challenges does Paul hurl at Timothy? 6:11-16. In his tremendous earnestness Paul here rises to heights of eloquence. His whole Epistle is a most impressive rebuke to indifference and carelessness in regard to affairs of the kingdom of God.

11. What application of Christianity to social problems does Paul make? 6:17-19.

12. What final charge does Paul give to Timothy? 6:20-21. He is greatly concerned that Timothy shall be preserved from the false teachings surrounding him on every hand and be kept in the true faith.

13. Note the closing benediction of grace.

NOTABLE PASSAGES IN I TIMOTHY

Paul the chief of sinners. Chapter 1. God's universal will for salvation. Chapter 2.

CHAPTER LXVII

II Timothy: Zeal in the Ministry

OCCASION.—This is Paul's last recorded letter. Imprisoned in Rome for the second time, he was momentarily expecting a martyr's death. Reports about lack of Christian zeal on the part of Timothy and other Christians troubled him greatly. This letter contains, therefore, a solemn charge to courageous and steadfast witnessing and to the endurance of hardship as "a good soldier of Jesus Christ." At the same time Paul feels very lonely because many have deserted him, and he urges Timothy to come to visit him. According to tradition, Timothy complied with this request and remained with Paul until his death. This Epistle has been called "Paul's swan-song."

OUTLINE OF II TIMOTHY

Theme: Zeal in the Ministry				
Salutation 1:1-2	A Charge to be Zealous 1:3—2:13	Faithfulness in Times of Apostasy 2:14—4:5	Paul's Last Messages 4:6-18	Greetings and Benediction 4:19-22

STUDY SUGGESTIONS

I. SALUTATION. Chapters 1:1-2.

1. How does Paul describe his apostleship? 1:1.
2. What does he call Timothy? 1:2.

II. A CHARGE TO BE ZEALOUS. Chapters 1:3—2:13.

1. What is Paul's cause of rejoicing in connection with Timothy? 1:3-5.
2. In what spirit is Timothy to carry on his ministry? 1:6-7.
3. What might he learn from Paul's example? 1:8-14.
4. What sorrows and joys had Paul experienced at the hands of his friends? 1:15-18.
5. What high ideals does Paul set before Timothy for the conduct of his office? 2:1-5.
6. What encouragement does he give? 2:6-13.

III. FAITHFULNESS IN TIMES OF APOSTASY. Chapters 2:14—4:5.

1. What instruction does Paul give concerning Christian teaching and living? 2:14-26.

2. What dreadful picture of the last times does he present? 3:1-9.

3. What should be the course of Christians in the presence of such evils? 3:10-17.

4. What are the chief elements in Paul's charge to Timothy? 4:1-5.

IV. PAUL'S LAST MESSAGES. Chapter 4:6-18.

1. In what spirit does Paul face death? 4:6-8.

2. What disappointments had he experienced? 4:9-16.

3. What does he long for? 4:9-13.

4. What was the source of his strength and confidence? 4:17-18.

5. Note Paul's friendly interest in the many persons to whom and from whom greetings are sent. 4:19-22.

NOTABLE PASSAGES IN II TIMOTHY

Timothy's spiritual heritage. Chapter 1. Enduring hardship as a good soldier. Chapter 2. Paul's finish of a good fight. Chapter 3.

CHAPTER LXVIII

Titus: A Bishop's Duties

OCCASION.—Titus was one of Paul's co-workers whom he appointed bishop of the church in Crete. On account of the serious weaknesses in the character of the Cretans the bishop faced many problems. It was for the purpose of instructing and guiding Titus in his difficult position that Paul wrote this Epistle.

OUTLINE OF TITUS

Theme: A Bishop's Duties			
Salutation 1:1-4	Duties As to Organization 1:5-16	Duties As to Teaching 2:1—3:11	Personal Matters and Greetings 3:12-15

STUDY SUGGESTIONS

I. SALUTATION. Chapter 1:1-4.

1. How does Paul describe himself?
2. What does he call Titus?

II. DUTIES AS TO ORGANIZATION. Chapter 1:5-16.

1. Why had Paul left Titus in Crete? 1:5.
2. What qualities should an elder (bishop) possess? 1:6-9.
3. Why was it especially necessary to have able elders in Crete? 1:10-16.

III. DUTIES AS TO TEACHING. Chapters 2:1—3:11.

1. What various groups of people does Paul mention as needing sound instruction? 2:1-10.
2. What ideals does Paul suggest for them?
3. What should motivate right Christian living? 2:11-15.
4. What relationship between faith and works does Paul point out? 3:1-8.
5. What final admonitions does Paul give? 3:9-11.

IV. PERSONAL MATTERS AND GREETINGS. Chapters 3: 12-15.
1. What requests does Paul make? 3:12-13.
2. What summary of Christian duties is given in 3:14?

NOTABLE PASSAGE IN TITUS

A catalog of Christian virtues. Chapter 2.

CHAPTER LXIX
Philemon: Appeal for a Slave

OCCASION.—Philemon was a well-to-do man in Colosse in Asia Minor, who had been converted to Christianity through the ministry of Paul. He was also a slaveholder. One of his slaves, Onesimus, had run away and eventually come to Rome, where he came into contact with Paul and became a Christian. The problem of his relationship to his master then became actual. Paul advised him to go back, but sent with him this letter in which he intercedes with Philemon for Onesimus and asks him to receive his former slave as a brother. According to tradition Philemon complied with this appeal and set him free.

This Epistle touches, therefore, on the relationship of Christianity to slavery. With Paul spiritual freedom was the chief concern; civil liberty was secondary. Consequently, he did not launch any revolutionary anti-slavery movement. The time was far from ripe for that. One-half of the population of the Roman empire was in slavery. But the principle of civil liberty is inherent in the very genius of Christianity and appears often in Paul's writings, as in the present Epistle. Ultimately, therefore, slavery was doomed in the presence of the onward march of Christianity, although the consummation of civil liberty did not take place generally throughout the world until our own day. And even now there are localities where the cause of civil liberty has not completely triumphed.

OUTLINE OF PHILEMON

Theme: An Appeal for a Slave		
Salutation and Thanksgiving 1-7	Argument and Appeal for Pardon and Reception As a Brother 8-21	Greetings and Benediction 22-25

217

STUDY SUGGESTIONS

I. SALUTATION AND THANKSGIVING. 1-7.

1. What do you learn about Paul's situation at this time?
2. To whom is the letter addressed? 1-2.
3. Note how graciously Paul expresses appreciation of Philemon's Christian qualities. 4-7.

II. ARGUMENT AND APPEAL FOR PARDON AND RECEPTION AS A BROTHER. 8-21.

1. Instead of making a demand upon Philemon, what does Paul do? 8-10.
2. What do you learn about the relationship between Paul and Onesimus? 10-14.
3. What treatment of Onesimus by Philemon does Paul suggest? 15-17.
4. What generous offer does Paul make? 18-19.
5. What do you think he intimates in v. 21?

III. GREETINGS AND BENEDICTION. 22-25.

1. What hope does Paul voice in v. 22?
2. From what associates does Paul send greetings? 23.

NOTABLE PASSAGES IN PHILEMON

The servant to be regarded as a brother. 15-16.

CHAPTER LXX

Hebrews: Christianity Superior to Judaism

NAME.—*The Epistle to the Hebrews* is so named from the very evident fact that it was intended especially for Jewish readers.

AUTHOR.—The writer of this Epistle is not known. Many Bible scholars believe that Paul was the author but did not attach his name to it because of prejudice against him on the part of many Hebrews. Other scholars hold that the ideas are Paul's, but that the writing was by some other Christian leader. At any rate, its thoughts are in complete accord with the theology of Paul.

TIME OF WRITING.—Probably about 63 A. D.

OCCASION.—On account of persecution and false guidance many of the Jewish Christians were apparently tempted to give up Christianity and go back to Judaism. In this Epistle, therefore, the writer most clearly, forcefully, and convincingly sets forth the superiority of Christianity over Judaism and urges the readers to hold fast to the Christian faith. Taking up, step by step, the elements in the Jewish religion, the writer shows in every case how the doctrines of Christianity are "better than" the old positions. The Epistle is, therefore, an exceedingly illuminating exposition of the meanings of the institutions, rites, and types of the Old Testament—the shadows of the things to come in Christ and His Gospel.

Theme: *Christianity Superior to Judaism*				
Introduction God Speaking Through the Prophets and His Son 1:1-4	Doctrinal Christ Superior to Angels, Moses, Joshua, and Priests 1:5—7:28	New Covenant Superior to the Old in Its Nature and Ordinances 8:1—10:18	Practical Exhortations to Hold Fast by Faith to the New Covenant 10:19—12:29	Conclusion Exhortations, Greetings and Benediction 13

STUDY SUGGESTIONS

I. Introduction. Chapter 1:1-4.

1. Note the absence of the name of the sender as well as any reference to the people addressed. In these respects the letter is different from others.

2. What is said about the relationship between God and His Son? 1:1-3. Cf. John 1:1 and 14.

3. Note the statement of Christ's exaltation. 1:3-4.

II. Doctrinal Section. Chapters 1:5—10:18.

A. Christ superior to angels. 1:5—2:18.

1. How does the author show that Christ is superior to angels? 1:5—2:18.

Note. Angels are referred to because they are the highest of God's created beings, and they came as God's representatives to men on various occasions in Old Testament times. But Jesus is far superior to these both in His nature and office as revealer of God.

2. Since Christ is so superior to angels, what attitude should men take to Him and His words? 2:1-4.

B. Christ superior to Moses and Joshua. 3:1—4:13.

1. How is Christ greater than Moses? 3:1-6.

2. What warning is given in 3:7-19?

3. What does the acceptance of the Gospel do for believers that Joshua did not accomplish for his people? 4:1-13.

C. Christ superior to the priests. 4:14—7:28.

1. What is said of Jesus as a high priest in 4:14—5:10?

2. What does the writer complain of in the readers, and what does he urge upon them in 5:11—6:20?

3. What is the significance of the statement regarding Christ that He was to be a high priest "after the order of Melchizedek"? Cf. 7.

Note. Melchizedek is more or less of a mysterious figure. All we know about him is what is stated here, in Genesis 14:18-20, and in Psalm 110:4. He is a striking type of Christ in several respects:

a) He was king "of righteousness" and "of peace."

b) He was superior to Abraham, for Abraham received a blessing from him and gave him tithes.

c) He was not of the Levitical tribe, but was given his double office directly by God. That Christ came as the fulfilment of the type prefigured by Melchizedek makes clear that He is superior to the Levitical priesthood, for ne holds His double appointment as high priest and king not by Levitical descent but by direct action of God and was greater even than father Abraham from whom the entire priesthood line descended. This is in brief the argument in Chapter 7.

D. The new covenant superior to the old. Chapter 8.

1. What is the relationship between the old Law covenant and the new Gospel covenant? Chapter 8. Note especially v. 2, 5-7 and 10.

E. The old tabernacle but a shadow. 9:1-10.

1. Why does the author go into detail about the old tabernacle? 9:1-10.

2. What were its deficiencies? 9:8-10.

F. Christ's the final and perfect sacrifice. 9:11—10:18.

1. What did Christ offer? 9:11-12.

2. What differences are there between Christ's sacrifice and those of the old covenant? 9:13—10:18.

3. Why was Christ's sacrifice effective and sufficient? Note especially 9:14; 9:24; 10:12-14.

III. PRACTICAL SECTION: EXHORTATIONS TO HOLD FAST BY FAITH TO THE NEW COVENANT. Chapters 10:19 —12:29.

1. What gracious privilege does the author urge his readers to make use of? 10:19-25.

2. What solemn warning does he give in 10:26-31?

3. To what hardships does he refer in 10:32-39?

4. What is the author's purpose in his masterly picturing of the triumphs of faith in past ages? Chapter 11.

5. To what does the author compare the Christian life in 12:1-2?

6. What is the value of suffering? 12:3-13.

7. What fruits of sanctification does the author set forth as desirable? 12:14-17.

8. What lessons do you derive from the comparison in 12:18-29?

IV. CLOSING EXHORTATIONS AND GREETINGS. Chapter 13.

1. What classes of Christian virtues does the author enjoin upon his readers? 13:1-17.

2. For what does he urge them to pray? 13:18-19.

3. Note the richness of content in the beautiful benediction in 13:20-21.

4. What do you note in the closing verses, 22-25?

NOTABLE PASSAGES IN HEBREWS

Christ the final revelation of God. Chapter 1:1-4. Christ the perfect High Priest. Chapters 4 and 5. Christ the Mediator of our salvation. Chapter 9. The nature and triumphs of faith. Chapter 11. The "cloud of witnesses." Chapter 12.

CHAPTER LXXI

The General Epistles

The seven Epistles following Hebrews are called the *General Epistles* because they were intended for the churches in general. Facts about these General Epistles may be set forth in tabular form as follows:

THE GENERAL EPISTLES

Name	No. of Chapters	About the Writer	Time of Writing	Sent from	Written for
James	5	An Apostle	About 60	Jerusalem	Hebrew Christians
1 Peter	5	An Apostle	About 64	Rome (?)	Christians in Asia Minor
2 Peter	3	An Apostle	About 67	Rome	Christians in Asia Minor
1 John	5	An Apostle	About 97	Ephesus	Christians in Asia
2 John	1	An Apostle	About 97	Ephesus	"The elect lady"
3 John	1	An Apostle	About 97	Ephesus	"Gaius, the beloved"
Jude	1	An Apostle	About 65	Jerusalem	Christians in General

CHAPTER LXXII

James: The Demonstration of Faith

OCCASION.—There seemed to have developed among some early Christians a tendency to think that because salvation is by faith in the merits of Jesus Christ, it was a matter of more or less indifference how they lived. This attitude James sternly rebukes in his Epistle. He says very pointedly that "faith without works is dead" and urges upon all Christians to show their faith by their works. There is no conflict with Paul's doctrine that salvation can not be earned by good works. Rightly understood Paul and James are in perfect accord. "Paul holds that faith leads to work; James that works must demonstrate faith." (Norlie)

OUTLINE OF JAMES

Theme: The Demonstration of Faith					
Salutation Chapter 1:1	By Patience in Temptation Chapter 1:2-27	By Deeds of Mercy Chapter 2	By Control of Tongue Chapter 3	By Purity of Character Chapter 4	Closing Exhortation Chapter 5

STUDY SUGGESTIONS

I. SALUTATION. Chapter 1:1.

1. How does James speak of himself? 1:1.
2. To whom is this letter addressed? 1:1.

II. DEMONSTRATION OF FAITH BY PATIENCE IN TEMPTATION. Chapter 1:2-27.

1. What values may be derived from temptation? 1:2-4.
2. What importance does James attach to faith in connection with prayer? 1:5-8.
3. How does James picture the transitoriness of riches? 1:9-11.
4. What are the roots of temptation and sin? 1:12-18.
5. How may victory over sin be attained? 1:19-27.
6. What definition of pure religion is given in 1:27?

III. Demonstration of Faith by Works. Chapter 2.

1. What relationship should exist among Christian brothers? 2:1-13.

2. What relationship should exist between faith and works? 2:14-26.

IV. Demonstration of Faith by Control of Tongue. Chapter 3.

1. Why is the control of the tongue extremely important? 3:1-12.

2. What are the marks of true wisdom? 3:13-18.

V. Demonstration of Faith by Purity of Character. Chapter 4.

1. What particular sins does James warn against? 4:1-12.

2. In what attitude should a Christian approach future undertakings? 4:13-17.

VI. Closing Exhortations. Chapter 5.

1. What judgment upon the wicked rich does James proclaim? 5:1-6.

2. How does he inculcate the virtue of patience? 5:7-11.

3. Note how solemnly he warns against swearing. 5:12.

4. What remarkable effects of prayer does he set forth? 5:13-18.

5. What blessings accompany the conversion of an erring brother? 5:19-20.

Notable Passages in James

Hearing and doing. Chapter 1. Faith and works. Chapter 2.

CHAPTER LXXIII

I Peter: Christians in Times of Persecution

OCCASION.—The churches in Asia Minor were face to face with persecution in many forms. It often meant loss of reputation, property, and even life to be a Christian. Many of them were, therefore, sorely discouraged. Peter, the "Apostle of Hope," in this Epistle strives to comfort them by reminding them of their precious inheritance as the children of God. He also shows the value of trials in the purging and strengthening of their faith.

OUTLINE OF I PETER

Theme: Conduct of Christians in Times of Persecution			
Salutation and Thanksgiving 1:1-12	Christians' Relation to God—Holiness 1:13—2:10	Christians' Relation to the World—Right Conduct 2:11—4:11	Exhortations, Greetings, and Benediction 4:12—5:14

STUDY SUGGESTIONS

I. SALUTATION AND THANKSGIVING. Chapter 1:1-12.

1. To whom is this letter addressed? 1:1.
2. How does Peter describe them? 1:1-2.
3. What seems to be uppermost in Peter's expression of thanksgiving? 1:3-5.
4. What idea is capable of sustaining the Christians in their trials? 1:6-9.
5. What precious promises had been fulfilled for the Christians? 1:10-12.

II. CHRISTIANS' RELATION TO GOD—HOLINESS. Chapters 1:13—2:10.

1. What idea of perfection is set before the Christians? 1:13-16.
2. What had been the cost of their redemption? 1:17-21.
3. From what source had new life come to them? 1:22-25.
4. Into what high station had the Christians been brought? 2:1-10.

226

III. CHRISTIANS' RELATION TO THE WORLD—RIGHT CONDUCT. Chapter 2:11—4:11.

1. What ideal of clean living is set forth? 2:11-12.
2. What ideal of citizenship? 2:13-17.
3. What ideal for servants? 2:18-25.
4. What ideals for wives and husbands? 3:1-7.
5. What ideals for Christians in general? 3:8-12.
6. What ideals for times of suffering and persecution? 3:13-22.
7. What is the perfect ideal? 4:1-6.
8. How should the thought of "the end of all things" affect the Christians? 4:7-11.

IV. CONCLUDING EXHORTATIONS, GREETINGS, AND BENE- DICTIONS. Chapters 4:12—5:14.

1. In what spirit is persecution to be met? 4:12-19.
2. What exhortations are given to elders? 5:1-4.
3. What to the people? 5:5-11.
4. From whom are greetings sent? 5:12-14.

NOTABLE PASSAGES IN I PETER

An incorruptible inheritance. Chapter 1. A holy nation. Chapter 2. Humility and trust. Chapter 5.

CHAPTER LXXIV

II Peter: Christians in Relation to False Teachings

OCCASION.—In addition to trials because of persecution, the Christians in Asia Minor were subject to dangers in the form of false doctrines, particularly, it seems, in regard to Christ's Second Advent. Peter, therefore, writes his second letter, some years later than the first, to instruct the people and to exhort them to be on guard against the false prophets.

OUTLINE OF II PETER

Theme: Christians in Relation to False Teachings			
Salutation 1:1-2	Exhortations to Progress in the Christian Life 1:2-21	Warnings Against False Teachings 2	Instruction Regarding Second Advent 3

STUDY SUGGESTIONS

I. SALUTATION. Chapter 1:1-2.

1. To whom is this letter addressed? 1:1.
2. What does Peter bespeak for them? 1:2.

II. EXHORTATIONS TO PROGRESS IN THE CHRISTIAN LIFE. Chapter 1:2-21.

1. What virtues does Peter look for in the Christians? 1:2-11.
2. What solemn admonitions does Peter give in view of his approaching death? 1:12-21.

III. WARNINGS AGAINST FALSE TEACHERS. Chapter 2.

1. How does Peter describe the false prophets? 2:1-3.
2. How does he prove their sure destruction? 2:4-11.
3. What catalog of sins does Peter charge against them? 2:12-22.

IV. Instruction Regarding the Second Advent.
   Chapter 3.

1. What particular reason does Peter give for writing his two letters? 3:1-7.

2. How does Peter explain the Lord's delay in coming back? 3:8-9.

3. How does Peter describe the "day of the Lord"? 3:10-13.

4. Anticipating the Lord's return, how should the Christians conduct themselves? 3:14-18.

Notable Passage in II Peter

The inspiration of Scripture. Chapter 1:16-21.

CHAPTER LXXV

I John: The True Nature of Christianity

OCCASION.—Christians in Asia for whom John carried responsibility were being subjected to false teachings in regard to the nature of Christ and the character of the Christian life. The Apostle, therefore, late in the first century, wrote this letter emphasizing the great truth that Christ is the revelation of God as light and love and urging Christians to live spiritual lives in the strength of fellowship with Him. Right faith and living will bring victory and joy.

OUTLINE OF I JOHN

Theme: The True Nature of Christianity			
Introduction: Nature of Letter 1:1-4	God Is Light: Live in the Light 1:5—2:28	God Is Love: Live in Love 3-4	Conclusion: Victory and Eternal Life Through Faith 5

STUDY SUGGESTIONS

I. INTRODUCTION. Chapter 1:1-4.

1. What points of comparison are there between this introduction and John 1:1-14?
2. What was the source of John's knowledge? 1:1-3.
3. What is the central idea in his message? 1:3-4.

II. GOD IS LIGHT: LIVE IN THE LIGHT. Chapters 1:5—2:28.

1. What is said about the nature of God? 1:5.
2. How do we demonstrate our fellowship with Him? 1:6-7.
3. What should be the Christians' attitude toward sin? 1:8-10.
4. On what basis does our assurance of the forgiveness of sins rest? 1:9—2:2.
5. What is the test of our Christianity? 2:3-6.
6. What is the heart of the Commandments? 2:7-11.
7. What were John's reasons for writing to the different groups? 2:12-14.

8. What should be the Christians' attitude to the world? 2: 15-17.

9. Against whom does John warn in 2:18-23?

10. What is the distinguishing mark of the anti-Christ? 2:22-23.

11. How may Christians best fortify themselves against false teachings? 2:24-29.

III. GOD IS LOVE: LIVE IN LOVE. Chapters 3-4.

1. Into what wonderful privileges do Christians come? 3:1-2.

2. What should be the results in their lives as far as sin is concerned? 3:3-12.

3. What positive Christian quality should dominate? 3:13-18.

4. Even if as Christians we realize our imperfections, what comfort may we have? 3:19-24.

5. How may Christians detect the Spirit of God and the spirit of the anti-Christ? 4:1-6.

6. How has God's love to us been most clearly demonstrated? 4:7-10.

7. In the light of this love what should be our relation to our fellowmen? 4:11-21.

IV. VICTORY AND ETERNAL LIFE THROUGH FAITH IN CHRIST. Chapter 5.

1. For whom are victory over the world and the obtaining of eternal life assured? 5:1-12.

2. How does union with Christ affect our prayer life? 5:13-17.

3. What is the ground of the Christian's final assurance? 5:18-21.

NOTABLE PASSAGES IN I JOHN

Assurance of forgiveness of sins. Chapter 1. Love not the world. Chapter 2. Blessedness of God's children. Chapter 3. God is love. Chapter 4. Victory through faith in Christ. Chapter 5.

CHAPTER LXXVI

II John: Attitude Toward False Teachers

OCCASION.—The fact that this letter is addressed to "the elect lady" has raised the question whether a particular individual is meant or whether the expression "elect lady" is a symbolic designation of a congregation. In either case the "household" concerned is commended for walking in the truth and exhorted to have nothing to do with false teachers.

OUTLINE OF II JOHN

Theme: Attitude Toward False Teachers		
Salutation 1-3	Thankfulness for Those Who Walk in Truth, and Warning Against Deceivers—4-11	Conclusion and Greeting 12-13

STUDY SUGGESTIONS

I. SALUTATION. 1-3.

1. What does John call himself? 1.
2. To whom is the letter addressed? 2.
3. About what is John chiefly concerned in writing? How many times is the word "truth" mentioned in this salutation?

II. THANKFULNESS FOR THOSE WHO WALK IN TRUTH.

1. In what does John rejoice? 4.
2. What is central idea in right Christian living? 5-6.

III. WARNING AGAINST DECEIVERS. 7-11.

1. How may false teachers be detected? 7.
2. How should Christians guard against error? 8-9.
3. What attitude should be taken toward false teachers? 10-11.

IV. CONCLUSION AND GREETING. 12-13.

1. What hope does John express? 12.
2. From whom are greetings sent? 13.

CHAPTER LXXVII

III John: Christian Hospitality

OCCASION.—"Gaius, the beloved" is commended for having shown hospitality in a right Christian spirit to certain evangelists, while Diotrephes is sharply rebuked for his unfriendly attitude.

OUTLINE OF III JOHN

Theme: Christian Hospitality			
Salutation 1	Commendation and Well-wishing for Gaius 2-8	Rebuke of Diotrephes 9-12	Conclusion and Greeting 13-14

STUDY SUGGESTIONS

I. SALUTATION. 1.

1. What relationship existed between the writer and recipient of this letter?

II. COMMENDATION AND WELL-WISHING FOR GAIUS. 2-8.

1. What does John wish for Gaius? 2.
2. Why was John pleased with his conduct? 3-4.
3. What attitude toward Christian evangelists is commended? 5-8.

III. REBUKE OF DIOTREPHES. 9-12.

1. Of what had Diotrephes been guilty? 9-10.
2. What warning does John give? 10-11.
3. By contrast, what sort of man was Demetrius? 12.

IV. CONCLUSION AND GREETING. 13-14.

1. What intention does John express?
2. Note the gracious salutation.

CHAPTER LXXVIII

Jude: Apostasy

OCCASION.—The dangers of apostasy were constantly threatening among the early Christians. Evil-minded men were trying to lead them astray in matters of both faith and conduct. Jude, therefore, urges Christians to "contend earnestly for the faith which was once delivered to the saints" and to walk in harmony with their Christian profession.

OUTLINE OF JUDE

Theme: Apostasy			
Salutation and Purpose of Letter 1-4	Punishments for Apostasy in Past and Present 5-16	Duty of Contending Against Apostasy 17-23	Doxology 24-25

STUDY SUGGESTIONS

I. SALUTATION AND PURPOSE OF LETTER. 1-4.
  1. What does Jude say of himself? 1.
  2. How does he describe those to whom he writes?
  3. What was the occasion for writing? 3-4.
  4. What does Jude urge upon the readers? 3.

II. PUNISHMENTS FOR APOSTASY IN THE PAST AND THE PRESENT. 5-16.
  1. List the historical illustrations of punishment for unfaithfulness. 5-16.
  2. What sober reflections do these instances of God's judgment suggest?

III. DUTY OF CONTENDING AGAINST APOSTASY. 17-23.
  1. What prophecies have been made regarding the last times? 17-19.
  2. What advice does Jude give? 20-23.

IV. DOXOLOGY. 24-25.
  1. How is God magnified in this doxology?

NOTABLE PASSAGE IN JUDE
Contending for the faith. V. 3.

234

CHAPTER LXXIX

Revelation: The Church Militant and Triumphant

NAME.—This book derives its name from the fact that it records a very remarkable *revelation* of "the things which are and the things that shall come to pass hereafter." It is also sometimes called the *Apocalypse,* from a Greek word meaning to *uncover* or *disclose.*

AUTHOR.—John the Apostle.

TIME OF WRITING.—About 95 A. D.

NUMBER OF CHAPTERS.—22.

CONTENTS.—The Book of Revelation gives a record of a series of visions which John had while in exile on the island of Patmos, in the Aegean Sea. In the visions John is given a message to each of seven churches in Asia Minor, setting forth reasons for which they are commended as well as grounds for rebuke, and exhortations to repentance, earnestness, and steadfastness. In the second group of visions the Apostle is given glimpses into the future of the Church and of the kingdom of Christ.

The visions are extremely rich in Oriental imagery and have given rise to the most varied speculations as to their meaning. There have arisen in the course of time various schools of interpretation, none of which may be said to hold the field exclusively at the present time. An idea on which many Bible scholars agree is that after certain events have come to pass in the history of the world and of the church the book will be much better understood than at the present time. However that may be, certain ideas that the book seems intended to teach may be set forth. Without going into detail in this brief survey, it seems clear that the visions deal with the career of the *militant and the triumphant church.* There is pictured the mighty conflict between truth and error, between the forces of righteousness and the forces of evil, between Christ and Satan, with the final complete triumph of Christ and His true church and the utter overthrow of Satan and his host. The final consummation of the plan of salvation takes place in the second coming of Christ, the execution of judgment, and the emergence of the new heaven and the new earth, of such glory as never entered into the imagination of any man.

The book of Revelation has, therefore, been a source of inspiration and encouragement to Christians in all ages, particularly in times of distress, trial, and persecution, and fills a large place in God's economy of revelation.

OUTLINE OF REVELATION

Theme: The Church Militant and Triumphant			
Introduction 1	The Church Militant 2-3	The Church Triumphant 4:1—21:5	Conclusion 22:6-21

Setting forth the divisions of this outline somewhat more fully, we note the following items:

I. INTRODUCTION. Chapter 1.

1. Inscription. 1:1-3.
2. Address and greeting. 1:4-8.
3. The occasion. 1:9-20.
a) Place and time of writing. 1:9-11.
b) Vision of Christ. 1:12-16.
c) Commission to write. 1:17-20.

II. THE CHURCH MILITANT. Chapters 2-3.

Epistles of commendation, rebuke, and admonition to the seven churches at Ephesus, Smyrna, Pergamum, Thyatira, Sardis, Philadelphia, and Laodicea.

III. THE CHURCH TRIUMPHANT. Chapters 4:1—22:5.

1. The opening of the seven seals. 4:1—8:1.
2. The sounding of the seven trumpets. 8:2—11:18.
3. The appearance of the seven mystic figures. 11:19—14:20.
4. The pouring out of the seven bowls of wrath. 15:1—16:21.
5. The judgment on Babylon. 17:1—19:10.

236

6. The last things: the advent of Christ, the overthrow of Satan, and the consummation of the kingdom of Christ in the new heaven and the new earth. 19:11—22:5.

IV. CONCLUSION. Chapter 22:6-21.

1. Commendation of this book and prophecy of Christ's coming. 22:6-17.

2. Warning as to adding to or taking away from this book and prayer for Christ's coming. 22:18-20.

3. Benediction. 22:21.

NOTABLE PASSAGES IN REVELATION

The vision of Christ. Chapter 1. The letters to the seven churches. Chapters 2-3. The great white host. Chapter 7. The new heaven and the new earth. Chapter 21.

STUDY SUGGESTIONS

In reading and studying this book one should not be discouraged by failure to understand the meaning of all the visions in detail. Some day perhaps they will be better apprehended. Read and re-read the book, and its large and glorious truths will become more and more precious. Read Daniel in connection with it. Discriminating use of able commentaries will also be of assistance.

CHAPTER LXXX

In Retrospect

We started out upon our exploration of *getting acquainted with the Bible* with keen anticipations of discovering interesting and precious things. It is to be hoped, as we now look back over the course taken that we are more conscious than before of what wonderful treasures are contained in this sacred volume. If we have been prayerfully openminded and carefully observant, we have seen the wonderful works of God, the sins and failures as well as the gropings and aspirations of humankind, the wonderful ways in which God has directed the course of history, His marvelous plan of salvation visioned forth in prophecy and type, dim at first but growing steadily more clear, the fulfillment of the age-long plan in the redemptive career of Jesus Christ, the founding of the Christian church by the agency of the Holy Spirit, its growth, guidance, and direction in the midst of hostile elements without and within, and prophecies of the ultimate victory and glory of the kingdom of Christ.

We have paused along the way to contemplate passages of unusual beauty and spiritual significance; we have pondered upon some of the profound problems that have busied the minds of thoughtful men throughout the ages; we have found answers to the great questions of the race: Whence came we? Why are we here? Whither are we bound?

We have discovered the objects and methods of saving faith; we have been challenged by the moral standards set by God Himself; we have considered the harmony that should exist between Christian theory and practice, between doctrine and life.

It is to be hoped that some of the many truths we have surveyed have found lodgment in our own hearts; that Jesus Christ, who is the center and core of the entire

Bible, has become more precious to us, and that His will and program have become regnant in our lives.

It is to be hoped, too, that we have become so acquainted with the Bible that it will continue to be for us a more treasured companion in daily life, and that it will be permitted to provide us with nourishing strength for lives of sacrificial service, and lead us on to our eternal home.